WEAPONS OF WORDS

Also by Stephen Fleischman…

The Reporter, a novel

A Red in the House: The Unauthorized Memoir of S. E. Fleischman

Short Jabs to the Head: Snapshots of History: 2005-2007

Moose in the City—Toronto 2000

WEAPONS OF WORDS

Snapshots of History | 2007 – 2010

Stephen Fleischman

iUniverse, Inc.

New York   Bloomington

Weapons of Words
Snapshots of History 2007-2010

iUniverse books may be ordered through booksellers or by contacting:

iUniverse
1663 Liberty Drive
Bloomington, IN 47403
www.iuniverse.com
1-800-Authors (1-800-288-4677)

ISBN: 978-1-4502-3302-6 (sc)
ISBN: 978-1-4502-3303-3 (ebk)

Printed in the United States of America

iUniverse rev. date: 05/14/2010

For

Genevieve Celeste Ward
&
Milo Ward

Table of Contents

Afterword

Foreword
by Eric Bercovici

"We are the contemporaries of the difficult century."
Alexei Surkov

Indeed.

The Russian poet and war correspondent Alexei Surkov wrote those words during WWII, words that made the people listen. And today, we also find ourselves living in a difficult century and the words of Stephen Fleischman collected in this book also make the people listen.

Yes. Words still matter. Thoughts still matter, though in our contemporary society, all too often they have become diminished in value. The media was once composed of real journalists, men and women searching, digging for the truth of what was happening in our country and in the world. Women journalists like Janet Flanner, Therese Bonney, Dorothea Lange, May Craig and men like Edward R. Murrow, Ernie Pyle, John Hersey, Bill Mauldin, only to name a few on that long list. And on the Russian front there was Ilya Ehrenburg, Vassily Grossman and Natasha Bode. But that kind of journalism is long gone, both here and there. Over the past decade what now passes as reporting has, on many occasions, been reduced to retyping government propaganda handouts and presenting them as fact. And that is a tragedy.

Today, to find the best of journalism, the best of political commentary one now has to turn to the internet, to the blogs. It is there you will find courageous writers like Paul Craig Roberts, Louis Proyect and Barry Grey. And there you will find the words of Steve Fleischman. Steve, now in his 90s, remains as clear-eyed and as sharp as he has been throughout his long career. And still writing with wit and an enviable perspective of history. You will find no timidity or soft-balling here. Steve writes it as he sees it and, as you will see in this book, he is on the money every time. Not surprising because Steve once worked with Ed Murrow and Walter Cronkite and Eric Severeid and with many other famed journalists during his long career. And he knows what real journalism is.

And now, right now, is when real journalism is needed in this country. The rapidly growing reactionary fury in America, complete with threats of violence, naked racism and even shouts for a right-wing revolution is being treated by powder puff reporting. Even the most outrageous right-wing lies pass unquestioned in the corporate owned mass media. Reverse the situation. Suppose the progressives were behaving in this way. How would a suddenly energized self-righteous media report that story? It's not difficult to imagine.

It has been said that wars bring out the best in the journalists who cover them and that was certainly true once when there was truth and passion in their words. But it certainly hasn't been true in America since September 11th 2001. That's when the downward slide began, that's when opposing opinions became "anti-American." And that's when this country began to split apart. Just look at the state of Congress today, one side against the other.

Alexei Surkov once said about those reporters who just wrote whatever the Kremlin wanted, "You know what they call this? 'Casting shadows on the fence.'"

You'll find no shadows on these pages.

With the brilliant articles in this book, Steve Fleischman has hit another high mark in his career.

Start reading.

Kaneohe, HI
April 10, 2010

Preface

Tom Paine, pamphleteer in colonial America alerted the people to what the British were up to in their attacks on the colonies during the Revolutionary War. His "weapons of words" helped forge the colonists and bring about a new nation called the United States of America.

Today, these united states are on the brink of disaster, on a slippery slope toward fascism, with a fake electoral system, the media a paper tiger, a corrupted legal system, and a non-existent labor movement, emasculated by corporate power.

The violence has already begun; the illegal militias are on the march.

These are some of the snapshots of history in this book.

Can we do something about it with our "weapons of words"…?

Stephen Fleischman
Los Angeles
April 10, 2010

Jobs, Jobs and Socialism

What this country needs is a whopping 18 million new jobs – and a good 5-cent cigar.

The chances are we'll get neither. Everybody's talking about jobs, jobs, jobs –but everybody that's talkin' about goin' to heaven ain't goin' to heaven...

We've got a killer whale in Barack Obama and John Boehner (R-Ohio), Minority Leader in the House, is calling him a socialist. Boehner slammed Obama's budget proposal and his recently passed economic stimulus package as "one big down payment on a new American socialist experiment." Others joined in.

Senator Jim DeMint of South Carolina called Obama "the world's best salesman of socialism" and Senate Republican Leader Mitch McConnell of Kentucky leapt into the Obama-socialist bash-fest with his own epithets.

As with health care reform, there's an obvious answer to the problem of unemployment but no one in our Congress has the guts to go for it—a government works program. But we can't have that! That would be socialism!

1

So what's a good socialist president to do? The answer—look back to our great tradition of government work programs.

The Works Progress Administration (WPA) under the New Deal worked for Roosevelt when it was passed by Congress in the depth of the Depression in 1935. The Republicans railed against Roosevelt then, too, for his socialist ideas. He struck back by calling them "economic royalists". And millions of Americans were employed rebuilding the infrastructure of the country—roads, bridges, parks, airports. Even artists, musicians, actors and theatrical groups were funded by the WPA. To good effect. More popular culture in America. For example, "The Living Newspaper" brought forth Orson Welles. He gave us "Citizen Kane", the brutal portrait of the newspaper magnate William Randolph Hearst. It riveted everybody's attention on one of America's most powerful oligarchs.

The corporate oligarchy that runs this country today is made of the same stuff—various segments of capital within the infrastructure as well as high ranking government officials, members of Congress, parts of academia, and other elements within the society. The mainstream media, mostly owned by five major corporate conglomerates, controls most of what we see, hear, and read.

Just about every elected politician is in one corporate pocket or another. The political system is fueled by campaign contributions. Politicians need money to get elected and the special interests that give it to them gets a quid pro quo. Everybody knows that's the way the system works.

Chris Hedges, in his Truthdig blog (3-8-10) pulls no punches when he describes America today: "There are no constraints left to halt America's slide into a totalitarian capitalism. Electoral politics are a sham. The media have been debased and defanged by corporate owners. The working class has been impoverished and is now being plunged into profound despair. The legal system has been corrupted to serve corporate interests. Popular institutions, from labor unions to political parties, have been destroyed or emasculated by corporate power. And any form of protest, no matter how tepid, is blocked by an internal security apparatus that is starting to rival that of the East German secret police. The mounting anger and hatred, coursing through the bloodstream of the body politic, make violence and counter-violence inevitable. Brace yourself. The American empire is over. And the descent is going to be horrifying."

How do the progressive forces of a nation come together to keep that from happening? Must we wait for another Great Depression, with millions living in Hoovervilles, before the working and under classes get organized?

The oligarchs are smarter than that. They know they have to produce enough jobs to fend off the growing resistance and Barack Obama is their front man to accomplish their goal.

President Obama crawled out of the Milton Friedman den at the Chicago school of economics where economists still exhort laissez-faire and deregulated capitalism. They're still looking for that illusive "invisible hand".

"I'm a market man," Obama chortled when he threw his hat into the ring.

After another year in the doldrums, the country is well on its way to an apple sale. The economy is floundering and the administration is still trying to talk its way into new days of glory. The hunt for a way to produce jobs (without the danger of being called a socialist) is getting desperate. The president and the Democratic congress are spinning their wheels. The disenfranchised Republicans have no wheels to spin. They're fixated, as they always are, on cutting taxes for the rich.

What we're talking about here are the two faces of the same monster. The two-party system, finely tuned to maintain the fiction of a democratic atmosphere. The capitalist oligarchy uses one or the other party to bolster the corporate interests as political environments change. No third party interlopers allowed. If Obama doesn't cut the mustard, they'll make him a one-term president.

Nonetheless, the infrastructure of the country, today, is a shambles. We can certainly use a little of that WPA mojo.

Any presidential candidate that can take the bullies by the horns and take some new ideas to the people could well become the next president of the United States.

How the Corporations Broke America

They started with the labor unions.

The labor movement, in this country, was brought to its knees by the corporate oligarchy, feeling its oats, in the 1980s.

Labor had a great tradition of fight in this country, going back to the Knights of Labor, organized in 1869, right up to the organization of the Congress of Industrial Organizations, (CIO) a federation of unions that organized workers industrially from 1935 to 1955 when it merged with the AFL.

We had some flamboyant labor leaders, too—Gene Debs, "Big Bill" Haywood of the IWW, the great John L. Lewis. They fought for higher wages and a higher living standard for workers, and moved many of them up into the middle class. That's what was called "the American Dream".

But corporate America was out to get organized labor from the year one. They found a champion in Ronald Reagan.

The successful campaign against labor was kicked off by President Ronald Reagan when he broke the Air Traffic Controllers strike in 1981.

As Labor Consultant Ray Abernathy recalls it, Reagan, "aided and abetted by former president Jimmy Carter and then-president of the AFL-CIO Lane Kirkland, fired 13,000 striking air traffic controllers, permanently replaced them, and drove the bar of U.S. labor relations so deep into the ground that we've never recovered."

When the members of the Professional Air Traffic Controllers Organization, (PATCO) voted overwhelmingly to strike the government, Reagan reacted within 48 hours, fired the lot of them and ordered the FAA to hire permanent replacements.

Replacing strikers in this manner wasn't against the law, but it had always been considered an extreme act and rarely done. When strikes were settled, a way was usually found to rehire striking workers with full seniority and often with back pay. But not in this case.

Former President Jimmy Carter already had it in for the Air Traffic Controllers during his administration when he planned the recruitment of replacement workers on rumors of a strike.

Lane Kirkland, certainly a union man, as head of the AFL-CIO, was miffed that the controllers had not consulted him before striking. He formally ordered AFL-CIO unions not to get involved in supporting their fellow unionists, the Air Traffic Controllers.

This sent a strong message to the corporate oligarchy. You can attack labor with impunity.

Abernathy graphically describes the effect, "The practice of 'permanently replacing' striking workers quickly became standard operating procedure in private industry and helped employer after employer either face down strikes or break them. What Carter, Regan and Kirkland conspired to do suddenly made union-busting socially acceptable and empowered corporations to initiate brutal deunionization campaigns. Losses at the bargaining table begat losses in union elections, effective strikes began to vanish, and the demise of labor was in overdrive.

The next blow against labor was struck by President Bill Clinton with NAFTA and globalization. And he set the stage for George W. Bush and Barack Obama to continue the attack.

Dennis Kucinich called it right when he said, "'Outsourcing' is a process in which American jobs, mainly in technological fields, are contracted out to countries where wages are significantly lower. The typical salary for an American programmer is $70,000 a year. The typical salary for a programmer in India is $8,000 a year. U.S. companies are expected to ship 200,000 jobs a year to India in the near future, in pursuit of these lower wages, and we have already lost a significant fraction of our manufacturing jobs to countries overseas."

The third prong of the attack was the military. Make a militarist nation out of the country. And that's exactly what they've done. With a volunteer army and at least two wars going, they've jumped the defense (war) department to monster size.

President Barack Obama sent to Congress a proposed defense budget of $663.8 billion for fiscal 2010. The budget request for the Department of Defense (DoD) includes $533.8 billion in discretionary budget authority to fund base defense programs and $130 billion to support overseas contingency operations, primarily in Iraq and Afghanistan.

The proposed DoD base budget represents an increase of $20.5 billion over the $513.3 billion enacted for fiscal 2009. This is an increase of 4 percent, or 2.1 percent real growth after adjusting for inflation.

While war costs rise, Obama cannot get any of his social programs through Congress. The Health Care Reform Bill languishes in the Senator without much hope of passing, unless as a boost to the health insurance industry by mandating the inclusion of the uninsured.

Meanwhile, unemployment continues at ten percent or slightly below and home foreclosures are unrelenting. Stimulus packages don't seem to work as the administration talks of jobs, jobs, jobs —but does nothing to create them.

If the government were to directly create jobs through a works program as in New Deal days, and help rebuild the infrastructure of this country, that would be called "socialism" —and we can't have that.

So we will sit back and watch the corporations break America.

Beware the Predator

Senator "Chuck" Grassley (R) Iowa, roiled up over the proposal for a public option in the health reform bill, called government a "predator not a competitor".

Government has been called many names, good and bad. Predator. That's a new one.

If Chuck feels that way about government, why doesn't he get out of it? Resign from the Senate.

Government is a neutral thing. Government is simply the organization through which control or administration of a city or state is exercised. It is used in the service of the entire nation not for a few special interests.

The conventional wisdom is that government cannot operate as efficiently as private industry.

It's a classic myth, the result of years, decades, even centuries of brainwashing. The propaganda of capitalism. Keep the notion of "public options", government run programs, out of peoples' minds. Demonize them as "socialism".

After all, if the working class got the idea that they, through a socialized government, can manage the means of production as efficiently as the capitalists, they might decide to do just that.

Entrepreneurs don't like to tackle that problem head on. They don't attack government, per se. They attack "big government".

"Big government is bad" –the common disparaging cliché.

The badness of big government is often raised when discretionary spending is being considered for some program to benefit the people. It signifies taxes and rich people don't like to pay taxes. Let the middle and working classes pay them. Rich people favor *tax cuts*, remember? They loved George W. Bush for that.

The rich don't mind discretionary spending for increases in the defense budget, for wars against small and weak countries that can't fight back. This means big bucks for the arms makers and the parasitic corporations that thrive along with them.

We've amassed a 2 trillion dollar deficit on that kind of discretionary spending. But not one dime for a universal single-payer health care system. Medicare is like a bone stuck in the throat of the health insurance industry.

For some unexplainable reason, we, as a nation, must keep a totally useless gang of blood-sucking corporatists, called a health insurance industry, a thousand pound gorilla, on our backs.

Republicans have declared they will do anything to kill any health care reform legislation. Their cry is that the Democrats are trying to restructure one-sixth of the economy, "writing a bill that will affect almost every American, every business and every doctor and hospital in the country," reports The New York Times. (10-4-09) The Democrats say the challenges are daunting.

True, the challenges are "daunting". They might not be so daunting if we could elect a congress of honest people, legislators who can't be bought off by the health insurance industry; legislators who represent us instead of them.

Hasn't the government taken on daunting jobs before? How about Medicare and universal health care for all Congressmen and Senators?

And besides… what's wrong with restructuring the economy. Isn't it about time?

We should use San Francisco as a model.

Maria L. La Ganga reports in The Los Angeles Times (10.4.09) that over the last two years, three-quarters of San Francisco's uninsured adults have been enrolled in a public program that guarantees access to medical care called "Healthy San Francisco".

So far, more than 46,000 adults have been enrolled in this city-run universal health care plan, the first in the nation. It has received high marks in recent independent studies.

Patients receive preventive services and ongoing treatment for chronic conditions. Prescriptions are covered and so are hospital stays.

A unique feature of the plan, patients must pick a "medical home" out of a network of more than thirty public and private clinics, physicians groups and hospitals within the city limits. The idea is that patients get consistent care and the system avoids duplicating services. Kaiser Permanente, a major private HMO, just joined and plans to accept up to 3000 patients.

The program is funded in part by an employer mandate, a controversial component of the plans now under discussion in Washington for the federal health care reform bill.

San Francisco Mayor, Gavin Newsom, described the program as "a public option", "a strategy to provide health care regardless of your ability to pay, regardless of any pre-existing conditions".

The city's plan is government run and subsidized—a "public option"— and has not caused workers or employers to bail out of private insurance, another lesson for the national debate.

It might be a good idea for Chuck Grassley to drop everything, make a trip to San Francisco, and take a look at this predator. That might make him decide to resign from the Senate—or he may learn something that will help him complete a health care reform bill with a "public option" that will pass the House and Senate and be signed into law by President Barack Obama.

The Founding Fathers
and the Luck of the Draw

If Sarah Palin doesn't know who the Founding Fathers are, she's not alone—neither do most Americans.

To begin with, George Washington was not the first president of the United States—John Hanson was. Hanson became president under the Articles of Confederation, which was the first constitution of the original thirteen colonies, ratified in March of 1781.

George Washington, Commander of the Continental Army fought the British Red Coats to their defeat. As a result of Washington's strategy, his forces eventually captured the two main British combat armies at Saratoga and Yorktown, leading to the war's end in 1783.

Washington presided over the Philadelphia Convention taking place there because of the general dissatisfaction with the Articles of Confederation. The delegates from the thirteen colonies at the Convention drafted a new United States Constitution in 1787 and unanimously chose Washington to become the first President of the United States under that Constitution in 1789. He sought to create a nation capable of surviving in a world torn asunder by war between Britain and France who were always at each other's throats in their empire building.

Washington supported plans to build a strong central government and create a national bank. For his central role in the formation of the United States, he is often referred to as "the father of our country".

In creating the new nation, George had a little help from his friends. The Federalist Party, led by Alexander Hamilton supported him and Washington responded in kind. He occupied the presidency for eight years. His farewell address in 1796 will be remembered for its stern warning against partisanship, sectionalism, and involvement in foreign wars.

Barack Obama could take a lesson here.

Technically, the Founding Fathers were those delegates from the thirteen colonies who were the signers of the Declaration of Independence in 1776 and those who participated in framing and adopting the United States Constitution of 1789.

Historian Richard B. Morris names seven of them as the key Founding Fathers: Benjamin Franklin, George Washington, John Adams, Thomas Jefferson, John Jay, James Madison and Alexander Hamilton. These people, and other delegates to the Philadelphia Convention, were landed gentry, plantation owners and the elite of colonial America.

Some historians define the "founding fathers" as a larger group, including ordinary citizens who took part in winning American independence; even dirt farmers who would drop their plow or their scythe, grab their musket and join the rag-tag army of General George Washington to fight the Red Coats wherever they were.

But the key politicians and the delegates to the Continental Congresses and the Philadelphia Convention called the shots. There were about fifty-five of them. These delegates represented a cross-section of 18th Century American leadership.

While the fight for independence was happening in America, in England, the Industrial Revolution was booming right along. A more modern world had begun. As new inventions were created, factories followed soon thereafter.

Samuel Slater, who had been an apprentice in an English cotton factory, came to America. Once here, he reconstructed a cotton spinning machine from memory. He then proceeded to build a factory of his own.

Then came Eli Whitney's cotton gin. In a nation where cotton was king, the cotton gin (short for cotton engine) was a machine for getting seeds out of cotton, making slave labor significantly more productive.

Then came James Watt's steam engine. A new power source spun off a myriad of new industrial machines and the creation of new manufacturing plants. The owners became rich and ostentatious. The Industrial Revolution and Capitalism had arrived in America.

It was a boon for the 1787 delegates.

According to Wikipedia, the Internet Encyclopedia, at the time of the Philadelphia Convention, of the fifty-five or so delegates, thirty-five were lawyers or had benefited from legal education and thirteen of them were merchants.

There were six major land speculators, including Robert Morris.

Benjamin Franklin and ten others speculated in securities on a large scale.

Twelve owned or managed slave-operated plantations or large farms, including George Washington, James Madison, Benjamin Franklin and Thomas Jefferson—Thomas Jefferson who wrote this beautiful piece of prose—the Declaration of Independence:

"... all men are created equal, that they are endowed by their Creator with certain unalienable rights; that among these are life, liberty and the pursuit

of happiness, deriving their just powers from the consent of the governed. That whenever any form of government becomes destructive to these ends, it is the right of the people to alter or to abolish it, and to institute new government…"

Yet, Jefferson, who owned as many as 200 slaves, freed only two slaves in his lifetime and five in his will and chose not to pursue two others who ran away. I guess he believed in the old adage: Do as I say, not as I do.

George Washington and James Madison also owned slaves; as did Benjamin Franklin, who later freed his slave and was a key founder of the Pennsylvania Anti-Slavery Society.

Alexander Hamilton was opposed to slavery and with John Jay and other anti-slavery advocates, helped to found the first African free school in New York City.

These are your Founding Fathers, Sarah Palin. Can you pick a favorite now?

A Pound of Flesh

Interest and Profit.

They fought about it in Shakespeare's time.

Shakespeare wrote a play about it. A character emerged depicting the essence of it. Shylock in "The Merchant of Venice"—a portrait of capitalism, in the period of transition from the feudal system.

Can you take a pound of flesh and spill not a drop of blood? That was the restriction Portia, the self-proclaimed lawyer, tried to impose on Shylock in Shakespeare's play. The pound of flesh was the interest Antonio would have to pay if he didn't return the 3 thousand ducats he borrowed on time. Portia excoriated Shylock's capitalist greed while defending his right to be a Jew, in a time of intense anti-Semitism.

David M. Boje, Professor of Management at New Mexico State University, says of the play, "this is a critique applicable to today's global corporate model of financial capitalism …

"…Shakespeare brilliantly portrays a conflict between courtly (feudal) usurer's capitalism and bourgeois merchant's capitalism, the triumph of the new forms of adventuring over the old in the 16th century."

In those times, usury (excessive interest) or even a normally accepted amount was considered a very bad sin in certain Islamic and Christian nations. Today, it's the normal way of doing business and is one of the pillars of the capitalist system. Money making money.

However, money is only a medium of exchange. It has no intrinsic value. It replaces a barter system. All classical economists, including Adam Smith and David Ricardo, recognize some form of the labor theory of value where the value of a commodity is determined by the amount of labor-power that goes into producing it.

Karl Marx brought a new paradigm to the understanding of capitalism with the hypothesis that "profit is derived from the surplus-value that is extracted when workers put in more labor than is necessary to pay the cost of hiring their labor-power".

This led him directly to the concept of the class struggle, the relations of production between capital and labor. Capitalism can only exist through the exploitation of the working class.

We're in another period of transition, today—the next stage in our evolving economic system. Will it be socialism or something else?

Can we imagine a society where interest and profit do not exist?

Perhaps it was the road not taken when societies emerged from feudalism, with the lord dominant over the serf. Or even earlier, before the formation of class systems when human societies consisted of hunters and gathers, where members of the tribe were equal in some form of primitive communism.

Well, let's see. The first thing we'll have to learn, to achieve such a state on a higher level, is to bring out the best in people, not the worst—and to do that we must recognize that human nature is complex and is made up of both.

Compassion and a desire to serve one's fellow man is as strong a drive in people as is greed. For a society, the stratagem must be to make the common good the standard behavioral form. The competition is in doing the best for mankind—rather than, "as long as I get mine, the devil take the hindmost".

In the context of our country, in the failing state of capitalism, how do we save ourselves? Instead of making some pacts with the future, we are clinging to the failures of the past.

Our current attempts at health care reform are a good example.

In a show at providing universal health care for the nation, the people's representatives dare not let these toxic words—socialized medicine or public option—cross their lips. Apparently, governments are no longer here to help our citizens. Powerful corporate entities, known as the health insurance industry, a part of the oligarchy that runs this country, won't allow it. They literally own a good many of our Congressmen and Senators, enough of them to stop any kind of meaningful health care reform. Citizens are brainwashed into thinking that what helps the insurance industry helps them.

You can fool some of the people some of the time.

The rest of us are fighting back. The fight won't be complete until the money changers are driven from the temple. If you can live with the mixed metaphor, we, the people, must take back our Congress, elect legislators that will represent us, not the special interests. Then, we might feel that we have a government that works.

If not, history will do it for us.

Instead of "The Merchant of Venice", we will have to look to Shakespeare's "Macbeth" or "Richard III" for a more violent solution.

One way or another, in Marx's own words, "Capitalism will dig its own grave."

Envisioning an Exit Strategy

In President Obama's speech, Tuesday night, he envisioned an exit strategy from Afghanistan while announcing that he's sending 30 thousand more troops to General McChrystal's command in that country.

Is envisioning an exit strategy anything like fighting a virtual war?

In Google's free dictionary "envision" is defined as: to picture in the mind, to conceive of as a possibility. It gives as an example, "I can see a risk in this strategy".

I think the free dictionary has it right.

Obama's problem is, how do you keep a war going when there is no reason for it? Well, maybe there is a reason; the profits of the military-industrial complex that President Eisenhower warned us about.

We're coming to a crucial stage in the Afghanistan war. Escalate or get out. Obama is trying to have it both ways.

What we can envision is a Vietnam-like ending to this war. Experts have already warned us on numerous occasions that this war cannot be won militarily. There has to be some kind of political solution. Sorry Barack.

You took the job. You have to carry out the orders of the oligarchy. This is a necessary war to keep these corporate entities in business.

An oligarchy is defined by the same free dictionary as a form of government in which power effectively rests with an elite segment of society—from the Greek for "few" and "rule".

Modern democracies can morph into oligarchies when actual differences between viable political rivals are small and politicians' careers depend heavily on unelected economic and media elites.

Corporate oligarchies are formed when power is captured by a small, elite group of insiders or influential economic entities such as banks or industries, with little regard for constitutionally protected rights.

President Barack Obama is now the figurehead for America's corporate oligarchy.

Barack Obama is a man without a heart or soul but with great rhetoric, master of the platitude and the cliché. He picked Zbigniew Brzezinski, as one of his closest advisors upon taking office, a former National Security Advisor to President Jimmy Carter, known for his hawkish foreign policy and a reputed operative for the military-industrial complex; or maybe it was the military-industrial oligarchy that picked Obama.

Obama made his pitch, Tuesday night, to 4000 cadets of the US Military Academy at West Point.

He used all the threadbare reasons for this new escalation of the war; reverse Taliban gains, protect the Afghan people from attack, provide time for them to build their own military capacity, increase pressure on al Qaeda in Pakistan and so on. He seemed to be in a hurry to get through the speech, taking up only 37 minutes. The cadets didn't demonstrate much enthusiasm, applauding lightly only twice.

Obama envisioned the de-escalation beginning in 2011. Using the old saw again, he said it was time the Afghans took more responsibility for their country. So, was Obama able to eat his cake and have it, too? I don't think he was able to convince anybody. It was probably the poorest speech in his repertoire.

So where do we go from here? With the country in near economic free-fall, why doesn't our Dear Leader do something to fix this country and let the Afgans take care of themselves?

Actually, the Taliban is one of the political entities of Afghanistan, like the Republican Party in this USA. So why does Obama vow to "break the Taliban". He's using it as a scapegoat to keep the war going. He can certainly find something better to do, like make sure there is a public option in the new Health Care Reform bill working its way through Congress – or better still, fight for the Singer Payer Plan.

Norman D. Livergood says in "The New Enlightenment": "In actuality, the basic social structure of the United States consists of the production of armaments by the 'defense industry' and the destruction of armaments in fabricated wars."

"Wars are not 'caused' by a crisis such as Pearl Harbor or 9/11 or nonexistent weapons of mass destruction; wars are contrived for political-economic purposes by those in power."

War and Profits

We know why there are wars, and we've known it for a long time. Good wars, that is, necessary wars, not wars by powerful foreign invaders, wars that might threaten our country.

Everybody knows we're in the process of old-hat empire building, the kind designed by the British in the salad days of colonialism and for which they took hits around the world by the likes of George Washington and Mahatma Gandhi.

No lessons learned there. President Obama is about to make a momentous decision on Afghanistan. He has been mulling over, for the last few weeks, how many more troops he will be sending to McChrystal, to further his counter-insurgency in that country. Ten thousand? Eighty thousand? Whichever, it's a process of foregone futility. And everybody knows it. But the mainstream media, heavy with punditry, spends endless hours hashing over every detail. And you don't have to be a weatherman to know which way the wind is blowing. The propaganda circle from government handout to media coverage is complete.

These graphs are provided by The Center for Public Integrity whose mission is to produce original investigative journalism to make institutional power more transparent and accountable. Just an example at random:

The Top 100
PRIVATE CONTRACTORS IN IRAQ AND AFGHANISTAN, 2004–2006

You are viewing page 1 of 7...

Rank	Name	Amount
*	Unidentified Foreign Entities	$20,435,870,190
1	KBR Inc (formerly known as Kellogg Brown and Root)	$16,059,282,020
2	DynCorp International (Veritas Capital)	$1,838,156,100
3	Washington Group International Inc	$1,044,686,850
4	IAP Worldwide Services Inc (Cerberus Capital Management LP)	$901,973,910
5	Environmental Chemical Corp	$899,701,070
6	L-3 Communications Holdings Inc	$853,535,680
7	Fluor Corp	$736,853,200
8	Perini Corp	$720,859,110
9	Orascom Construction Industries (OCI)	$617,089,510
10	Parsons Corp	$579,265,450
11	First Kuwaiti General Trading And Contracting Company Wll	$495,404,500
12	Blackwater USA	$485,149,590
13	Tetra Tech Inc	$362,107,010
14	AMEC PLC	$317,171,280

Here's how the circle of influence works:

http://www.publicintegrity.org/assets/swf/090909_circle/

We elected Barack Obama to change all that, didn't we?

But Obama took over from Bush without missing a stroke. The faceless corporate oligarchy that runs this country has been around awhile. It ran Clinton and Bush, now runs Obama. (How far back do you want to take it?) Who are these oligarchs? Yes, there are factions within the oligarchy. They have their differences. They don't all agree. They represent different entities of industrial and corporate power. They have their collateral network. They are the pillars of capitalism. They are mostly unheard and unseen, but occasionally you may get a glimpse of a face…

Obamastocks.net says this:

Zbigniew Brzezinski - Puppet Master of Obama?

By admin
Topics:
Uncategorized

"Zbigniew Brzezinski is the puppet master of Obama. This is a fact. Brzezinski is an 80-year old man from Poland who despises Russia. He was behind the catastrophic Carter administration. Brzezinski has the ultimate plan of preventing China from gaining access to African oil. China must have access to African oil or else the Chinese economy will recess rapidly. Brzezinski figures this will force China to invade the oil rich fields of southeast Russia just above North Korea. If China were to militarily take these oil fields from Russia, the two would obviously be at war which is what Brzezinski seeks. That plan is perfect in his eyes as it will weaken those two super-powers thus enabling American imperialism to regain strength. The real problem with this plan is that the Russians and Chinese are well aware of it. They know what Brzezinski intends to do. Unfortunately, the end result will most likely back fire on the west and produce world war III—China and Russia against the US and Europe."

The strategy of George W. Bush to keep the nation in a state of perpetual war was to keep the American public in a state of fear. Obama is continuing that strategy. We must keep an enemy in the cross-hairs.

Al Qaeda, of course, is the one that does the trick—an Islamic group calling for global jihad. They claimed responsibility for 9/11—blowing up the twin towers of the World Trade Center in New York City—for blowing a hole in the USS Cole, for bombing US embassies in Africa. Al-Qaeda has attacked civilian and military targets in various countries. They have instilled fear in many places. When you hear the words "Al Qaeda", think bogeyman.

The demonizing of the word "terror" didn't originate with George W. Bush. Ariel Sharon, army general and a former Israeli Prime Minister, and others before him, used the technique quite effectively. They turned just about every Palestinian into a "terrorist" which put the mission of Zionism on the road to a Greater Israel.

Sharon's own government found that he bore personal responsibility for the Sabra and Shatila refugee camp massacre of Palestinians in September of 1982.

Acts like these notwithstanding, the United States has been a staunch ally of Israel and supporter, in this special relationship, through the years, despite its war-like moves against the Palestinians, the Gaza Strip and the adjoining country of Lebanon.

According to Kathleen and Bill Christison, writing in Counterpunch, the United States committed to giving Israel $30 billion over the next decade. The only stipulation to Israel's use of this cash gift is that it spends 74% of it to purchase U.S. military goods and services. Israel is, by far, the largest recipient of U.S. foreign aid.

Not bad for our war industry. We can keep our wars in Iraq and Afghanistan going, and then some.

Do you like the idea of your son or daughter giving his or her life for the profits of KRB or DynCorp International?

I don't think anyone could call that "service to my country".

The Tea-Party System

In the first Boston tea party, the colonists dumped the British tea into Boston Harbor because of taxation without representation.

The tea-baggers, today, are making a fracas because they want corporation representation without taxation.

Michelle Bachman, Congresswoman from Minnesota, also known as the "Crazy Lady", is leading the tea-bag movement against the health care reform bill right into the arms of the health insurance industry.

"It was Thomas Jefferson who said a revolution every now and then is a good thing," she says, as she slams a two-foot stack of paper representing the bill.

The main-stream media, as is its wont, is picking up the oligarchy's propaganda beat. The issue they're beating around the bush about now is the pubic option. Another issue is more de-troupes for Afghanistan.

The oligarchy is pushing the pundits, and the punditry is bringing out their big guns—David Gergel and Wolf Donner Blitzen. They have panels, too, with Leslie Stalled, Lucrezia Borgia and her sister Gloria, Keith Globerman and Rachel Rachel. They can talk a hatful.

AC-DC 360, Gloria Vanderbilt's son, has a firm grip on the teats of the cash cow at CNN. They know, over at Ted Turner's barnyard, that if you put an hour's worth of programming together, you can snowball that into a 24-hour news cycle on a cable-grable channel.

Over at 13th Century Fox, you've got Bill O'Piggy and his piglets, Insanity Hannity, Glen Beckish and Crispy Wallace under the aegis of Rupert In-The-Dock Murderock and Roger Beerandailes.

Now, Barney Obama, with his chief henchman, David Axelgrease, have an important decision to make and they're not making it. Will they, won't they, will they, won't they, will they send the troops?

You've got twenty four hours of prime time chawed right there. The military pundits, chief among them Armchair General Barry McCaffrey, head of the Joint Chiefs of Staff for NBC and MSNBC, are having their crack at it, too.

The profusion of talk about the pubic option coming up for a vote maybe next week or maybe not, is almost as good as Michael Jackson dying but comes nowhere close to the O.J. Simpson romp.

There were times when we used to have third parties kicking around; most recently, Monkey Wrench, Ralph Nader and his raiders. He kept running for president (of the United States, that is) and getting about 0.02% of the vote, giving the Democrats the perfect excuse for losing the election.

We had Texas business man Ross Perot, candidate for president in 1992 and 1996, the second time under the banner of the Reform Party, which got him absolutely nowhere, not even on the platform with the tea party candidates in the presidential debates.

In 1955, the Communist Party (CPUSA) finally dissolved because its membership consisted solely of FBI agents.

Ah, but there was a time when Third Parties struck!

Wikipedia says, "**Labor Party** was the name or partial name of a number of United States political parties which were organized during the 1870s and 1880s.

The **Social Democratic Workingmen's Party of North America** was formed in 1874. By 1877 the party changed its name to the Socialist Labor Party of North America, and continues under that name.

In 1877, the racist Workingman's Party was formed in California, led by Dennis Kearney; by 1879 it was powerful enough to help re-write the state constitution of California, inserting provisions intended to curb the powers of capital and to abolish Chinese contract labor.

In 1878, the Greenback Party, under the influence of leaders of organized labor, changed its name to the **Greenback Labor Party**, and continued to operate in some states, electing a congressman as late as 1886; but by 1888 had dissipated. In 1886, a **United Labor Party** was organized in Chicago under the leadership of that city's Central Labor Union; It drew over 20,000 votes for its county ticket in the fall of 1886, and in the following spring elections garnered 28,000 votes for its candidate for Mayor; but by 1888 it had merged with the Democratic Party in that city.

Theodore Roosevelt's Bull Moose Party split the Republican Party in 1912, long before Sarah Palin got around to it.

So, you see, there is still hope for America!

Foot in the Door

Isn't it perfectly clear that the uproar over a public option in the health care reform bill now squeezing its way through Congress is about nothing but the foot in the door to socialized medicine and ultimately to other socialized things?

What a break that would be when you look around and see what capitalism hath wrought. While the ice-caps melt, corporate America is making billions on the dooming of the planet.

Capitalism developed out of England's industrial revolution in the 18th Century. Today, it is a global phenomenon; multi-national monopoly capitalism.

Why have the people of the world let this happen?

The depredations of capitalism were known back in the 19th Century when Karl Marx made it perfectly clear that the system stinks and is only good for the rich and the bourgoisie and the working class gets screwed.

His definitive analysis of capitalism with the publication of his book, "Das Kapital" spilled the beans. Its first volume was published in 1867.

His warning goes back even further than that—to 1848 when he wrote "The Communist Manifesto".

John Molyneux, a British socialist, activist, and interpreter of Marxist theory explains it this way, "Capitalism is a mass of interlocking contradictions. The contradiction between the capitalist class and the working class is rooted in the exploitation that takes place in every capitalist workplace. The fact is capitalism cannot do without the working class; it needs it to produce its profits. And the more capitalism grows and expands, the more it is compelled to increase the size and potential power of its mortal enemy. The bourgeoisie can win battle after battle but it cannot win, or end, the war. The class struggle can end only with the overthrow of the bourgeoisie and the abolition of capitalism."

One of capitalism's meanest effects—the free market's assault on the environment—the one resource mankind cannot afford to lose.

A handful of parasites live off the backs of the workers. Every bit of the capitalists' vast wealth is stolen from working people. Workers get paid for only a part of what they produce. The surplus value that they create goes straight into the hands of the capitalists as profits.

A free-market ideology has no regard for human life; capitalist elites and their partners in the White House and Congress, turned the financial sector into a giant Ponzi scheme.

In the insurance industry, so far this year, 142 insurance merger deals have taken place in the U.S., with a total value of $5.3 billion, putting insurance tenth among all industries, according to Mergerstat, the leading provider of merger and acquisition statistics.

The U.S. health system accounts for a higher portion of the gross domestic product than any other country but ranks 37th out of 191 countries in its performance, the UN World Health Organization report finds.

The United Kingdom, which spends just six percent of GDP on health services, ranks 18[th.] Several small countries – San Marino, Andorra, Malta and Singapore are rated close behind second-placed Italy.

But it seems people still haven't gotten it.

Since the era of Ronald Reagan, 40th president of the United States, (1981-1989), the labor movement in America has slowly but inexorably been whittled away.

"Reaganomics", the name for President Ronald Reagan's supply-side economics, basically deregulated corporations and granted tax cuts for the rich.

The rest of the country suffered and still suffers. Millions of Americans have lost their jobs; millions are threatened with loss of their homes; millions have seen their retirement funds melt before their eyes; millions are threatened with loss of health care. As Americans on Main Street are being devastated, executives of bailed out banks continued to receive billions in bonuses.

The working class is in a state of paralysis today. Corporate America has smashed the unions, bought out Congress and the Executive Branch and rules supreme. President Barack Obama, a creature of the corporate oligarchy, carries out their orders. His betrayal of the people who elected him is painfully obvious.

But the country is in a fragile state. With two senseless and futile wars sapping our treasure and human resources for more than seven years and other wars continually threatening, the ruling elite faces an economic collapse.

Turning the nation into a militarized state seems the only way to keep it going.

With that famous phrase "military-industrial complex", used for the first time on January 17, 1961, President Eisenhower warned, "In the councils of government, we must guard against the acquisition of unwarranted influence, whether sought or unsought, by the military industrial complex. The potential for the disastrous rise of misplaced power exists and will persist…"

Capitalism is, again, facing its eternal contradiction.

Is this what the members of Congress, fighting the "public option", fear most—the erosion of capitalism and that foot in the door to some form of socialism, or maybe just some good old democracy?

Socialism may require a little more than that. The sweep of history.

Hypocrisy Unbridled

I learned my first lesson in capitalism when I was a kid during the Great Depression of the 1930s. (Yes, I was a teenager in 1933)

In our living room, we had only one electric light bulb. It hung down from the middle of the ceiling on an electric wire. My father insisted that when you left the room, even for a short while, you turned off the light. You don't waste electricity.

Every so often the bulb would blow out and have to be replaced. It was common belief, at the time, that the manufacturers could make an electric light bulb that would never blow out, but they wouldn't do that because they wanted to keep selling light bulbs. We believed that was true of other items as well. That's how capitalism worked.

I now know that it was called "planned obsolescence" and it was a well known and accepted tenet of capitalist marketing.

We're coming to the end of the road, now.

See where planned obsolescence has taken General Motors. It is one of the nation's iconic corporations that practiced it.

This was true of the auto industry in general. The new models appeared yearly, most of the time with nothing but cosmetic changes. The American consumer was programmed. A trade-in every year or two or three was "de rigueur", but when foreign cars started penetrating the American market, Mercedes, BMWs, Toyotas, Hondas, the American consumer wised up. Here were better products that lasted longer.

In later years, I learned other lessons about the contradictions of capitalism and the path it must take to its own destruction.

Going back to Adam Smith, the concept that the "invisible hand" of the free market would keep the capitalist economy in balance has been the conventional wisdom. Capitalism must grow or die. And grow it did. Mergers and acquisitions became the modus operandi as corporate enterprises struggled with their competitors to survive.

We have a world-wide economic system of monopoly capitalism, now, that is in a state of perpetual class struggle—capital vs. labor —or bourgeoisie vs. proletariat, as Karl Marx put it. Within it, the contradictions are legion—in all aspects of life, even within the context of one politician's speech.

Take this one, for example, that David Henderson of Econlog points out about the Obama health care speech to a joint session of Congress, last September 9th.

He's for a public option and against it within a single speech.

"These private companies can't fairly compete with the government," the President said. "And they'd be right if taxpayers were subsidizing this public insurance option."

"But they won't be," Obama continued, "the public insurance option would have to be self-sufficient and rely on the premiums it collects."

Then, two paragraphs later, he has "great concern" about how to pay for the government option. He states flatly that money will come out of Medicare and Medicaid. So, some of the money for a public option in the health care reform bill will come out of currently existing government health care programs. Is that a contradiction, or what!

Take Wall Street and Main Street. While the banks are making money again and bonuses are flying like hydrogen balloons, employment is dropping like a lead balloon. The government regulators are doing nothing about reinstating the Glass-Steagall Act of 1933 that established the Federal Deposit Insurance Corporation (FDIC) and separated commercial banks from investment banks. Like church and state, they don't go together unless you want a gambling casino. Glass-Steagall staunched the bleeding and was pivotal in saving the financial system after the Great Depression.

By 1999, the Wall Street fat cats forgot everything they learned from that period. Apparently, they wanted a gambling casino. Provisions that prohibited a bank holding company from owning other financial companies were repealed on November 12th by the Gramm-Leach-Bliley Act—that's Gramm as in Senator Phil Gramm, a practiced croupier at the craps table.

Wall Street went on a rampage, creating all kinds of financial gimmicks derived from derivatives you could bet on; things like packaged debt that they could bundle and sell in foreign markets and sub-prime mortgages that eventually put peoples' homes under water.

This is what put our country into financial crisis in 2008 when we had to socialize the debt and privatize the perpetrators.

When we elected Barack Obama, we thought we were going to get change we could believe in. But Barack put the same old foxes into the chicken coop—Summers and Geithner, the ones who presided over the disaster to begin with.

Just another contradiction of Capitalism.

We are yet to see anything like Glass-Steagall reinstalled or anything that resembles it; any kind of robust regulation of the Wall Street gambling joint.

Just hold your breath and cross your fingers. Maybe the scales will fall away from eyes. That's what scales usually do when truths become self-evident.

The Walrus and the Carpenter Are Talking Again

(With apologies to Lewis Carroll)

"...a properly resourced counter-insurgency probably means more forces," said Adm. Mike Mullen, chairman of the Joint Chiefs of Staff, before the Senate Armed Services Committee, "... more time and more commitment to the protection of the Afghan people and to the development of good governance."

"The time has come," the Walrus said, "to talk of many things: of shoes -- and ships – and sealing wax –of cabbages and kings ...

The Carpenter said nothing but, "cut us another slice..."

"Oh, Oysters, come walk with us. The day is warm and bright. A pleasant walk, a pleasant talk, would be a sheer delight. Yes, and should we get hungry on the way, we'll stop and, uh, have a bite."

"I weep for you," the Walrus said, "I deeply sympathize." With sobs and tears he sorted out those of the largest size...

The United States of America hardly sheds a tear when it destroys a nation. We always do it for the good of the people of that nation. We must protect them from themselves. We can't allow the Taliban to return to Afghanistan.

The Taliban happens to be an indigenous, religious and political movement that governed Afghanistan for five years when it was removed from power by US and NATO forces in 2001.

Whatever happened to self-determination?

In some strange way, the Taliban is being held responsible for 9/11.

In 2004, the Taliban reared its hoary head again, and started a strong insurgency, fighting a guerrilla war against the puppet government in Kabul and its US and NATO allies participating in "Operation Enduring Freedom"—the one Adm. Mullen was talking about.

Eight years of pounding is not enough. There is hardly a structure left standing, untouched.

We had to cause regime change in Iraq. Saddam Hussein was a threat to the United States with his weapons of mass destruction which he didn't have.

No matter.

"Little Oysters? Little Oysters? But answer there came none. And this was scarcely odd because they'd been eaten. Every one!"

Panama and Grenada were necessary wars. In Grenada, medical students were threatened, and Panama...well, Noriega came from there.

Korea was another matter. The North Koreans were being helped by Red China. Why were we there? I don't exactly remember.

Now, Vietnam! That was a war! That's where we learned about guerrillas—fighters who swim among the people like fish is water.

Not many people had ever heard of the place, down in South-East Asia somewhere. The country was split during World War II. The French colonialists held onto the south, Red China took the north.

We had dominoes back then. Vietnam was a domino. The domino theory had it that if South Vietnam fell, all of Southeast Asia would go Communist.

The French had been playing dominoes in Vietnam since before World War II. And when the war was over, the French came back to continue the game. But they found a guy there by the name of Ho Chi Minh who didn't like the idea, and he put up quite a fight. In fact, he beat the feces out of the French at a place called Dien Bien Phu. The French yelled "Help!" The US sent in the Marines and eventually took over the war, as it is wont to do. We couldn't let all of Southeast Asia go Communist, now, could we?

We should apply what we learned in Vietnam to what's happening in Afghanistan now. The Russians learned their lesson.

The one thing you can say for the war in Vietnam; it created the strongest anti-war movement America had ever known. It put a stop to the war. Nothing like that has been accomplished since.

The War Between the States—the US Civil War—Lincoln's war, you could call it, was a war to preserve the union, and incidentally, end slavery.

The official figure is that about 620,000 Americans perished in that war, in the four years between 1861 and 1865—360,000 on the Union side—258,000 on the Confederate side—more than in all other wars from the Revolution to Vietnam.

We live in a country that was born in genocide with the extermination of the Native American tribes, and we matured in a state of slavery to nourish the plantation system.

One hundred and fifty years later, racial antagonism is still a hallmark of this country. Now, with a black president, one would think that racism has relented, but beneath the surface the stench of it can be felt (or smelt).

When a Senator yells "liar" at our president during an address to a joint session of Congress; how do you interpret that? A civil war smoldering beneath the surface?

You be the judge. With a corporate oligarchy running the country, you can expect some fall-out.

Barack Obama knows how to handle himself in the clinches. He gets screaming applause when he mentions "public option" at a rally for health care reform, and boos when he mentions Senator Max Baucus, Democrat of Montana, head of the Finance Committee, that just put out a health care reform bill that would warm the cockles of the health insurance industry's heart (if it had one).

Obama knows how to maneuver and that's what the oligarchy likes and why he's in the job. You can be sure that there will be no "public option" in the bill that eventually passes.

And you can be sure that there will be more troops heading to Afghanistan, perhaps as many as 45,000, to join the 68,000 already there. You can bet your McChrystal on it.

Adm. Mullen tipped Congress off last Tuesday and if the Democrats oppose the request, they would be seen as flouting independent military advice.

"But Mother Oyster winked her eye and shook her hairy head. She knew too well this was no time to leave her oyster bed."

Does this mean that we are living in an Alice in Wonderland world?

The Federal Twist

We've been witnessing a torrent of twisted logic, lately, in the jousting over the Obama Administration's health care plans.

The Obama mantra seems to be that in order to get more health care we have to cut it.

This is scaring the pants off old people on Medicare and those in other government programs like Social Security, Medicaid for the poor, Veterans' programs and Champus, also called Tricare, providing health care to military families.

If Obama really wanted to cut health costs in order to afford universal health insurance, he would be screaming for the single-payer option that has been forced off the table by the clout of the insurance industry.

When he was a candidate for president, seeking your vote, Obama was all for the single-payer plan.

When elected, you saw a federal twist in action when he was joining in, rather than fighting off, the cabal. Now he is a well indoctrinated member of the corporate oligarchy.

He has continued just about every one of the Bush policies, foreign and domestic; not only his health care stance, but equally outrageous the continuation and escalation of the war in Afghanistan while war in Iraq drags on. Obama has even added something new with Af-Pak, which includes Pakistan in the package, and the killing of civilians with pilotless drones.

The tease about closing Guantanamo was just that, a tease, and another promise broken.

Boiling over on the front burner, right now, is the public health care option while keeping the single payer plan under the radar screen.

The way the single-payer health plan works, the government collects all medical fees and then pays for all services through a single government (or government-related) agency.

In Congress, H.R. 676, if passed into law, would replace private insurance companies with just such a publically managed insurance plan. It would prove how superfluous health insurance companies are. They pocket one-third of the money you pay them in premiums which is why they make such whopping profits and why they'll fight to the death to maintain the status-quo.

Why should there be people making money on your health?

Just about every civilized, industrial nation, and even some third-world countries, have government run health plans; Australia's Medicare, Canada's Medicare, and healthcare in Taiwan are examples of single-payer universal health care systems.

In contrast, socialized medicine would be a system in which all health personnel and health facilities, including doctors and hospitals, work for the government and draw salaries from the government, an example being the U.S. Veterans Administration, while U.S. Medicare is a single payer system which is not socialized medicine.

Under the British National Health Service, which also uses a universal single-payer fund, the public owns the health systems and facilities. The term single-payer thus only describes the funding mechanism—referring to health care being paid for by a single public body—and does not specify the type of delivery, or who doctors work for.

The term single payer does not imply a socialized medicine system.

Since Americans are so frightened by the word "socialism", this is one distinction they've got to get under their belts.

The majority of physicians in the United States are in favor of a national health insurance system. A recent study published in 2008 in <u>Annals of Internal Medicine</u>, a leading medical journal, showed 59% of physicians "support government legislation to establish national health insurance," while 32% oppose it and 9% are neutral.

This represented an increase of 10 percentage points as compared with a similar survey in 2002 in which support for such legislation stood at 49% of physicians.

Among the general U.S. public, recent polling ratings for single-payer are apparently dependent on how the question is asked, ranging from 49% to 65% in favor.

President Obama is taking a drubbing on the issue from those Blue Dog Democrats who should be stacked on the dead-wood pile along with the Republicans.

Blue Dog Senator Max Baucus, D-Mont., chairman of the Senate Finance Committee, working on a health care bill, made it clear that "the so-called 'public option' would not be part of any deal with his name on it."

Obama, though, so far has not said he will demand a public option. He also has not said he will veto a package that omits a government-run health insurance program. This late in the game, he is keeping everyone guessing.

But since Obama, himself, was on the take from the insurance industry fat-cats, he may wind up, as well, on the dead-wood pile if that public option doesn't get into the bill from Congress everybody is waiting for.

People are making book on whether it will or won't. If not, it's a no-win option for all Americans, another turn of the Federal Twist.

And I don't mean that pretty place near Princeton, New Jersey.

The Robber Barons Are Back

Actually, they've never left.

The predatory capitalists who stole big chunks of this country at the end of the 19th and early 20th Century were given the moniker "robber barons" and the name stuck.

In railroads, they were represented by such sharks as Leland Stanford, Charles Crocker and Mark Hopkins in the west, and Andrew Carnegie and Jay Gould in the east. The US government gave them huge swaths of public land on both sides of their rail lines as a reward.

In oil, it was John D. Rockefeller, of course, and Henry Flagler in New York and Florida; in steel, in addition to Carnegie there was Henry Frick and John Gates; in real estate and finance, John Jacob Astor and Daniel Drew; in tobacco, James Buchanan Duke in Durham, North Carolina; and so it went…

Not only did they get land and forests and other treasures but also the minerals beneath the surface, all of which are gifts of nature which should belong to all the people.

Yes, the capitalists built the means of production, but without wage labor the plants were useless. They regarded labor as a commodity to be bought; a glut on the market so its price was cheap.

A wage earner was paid just enough to keep him alive and to reproduce himself. The entrepreneurs needed to keep the supply of labor flowing for future exploitation. They were always able to squeeze the surplus value out of the working class.

When labor started to organize, form unions, collectively bargain and withhold their labor power in the form of strikes, they were able to keep a bigger piece of what they produced, raising purchasing power that benefited living standards for all.

Although global capitalism had the upper hand through most of its history, the class struggle (the fight between the haves and the have-nots) was always there. And it's there, today.

The health insurance-pharmaceutical-medical-complex has its robber barons operating in force, as does the Wall Street gang with Timothy Geithner and Lawrence Summers. The military-industrial and prison-industrial complexes have theirs as do other branches of capital.

The political ring-master is, of course, our president, Barack Obama, not only a man of charm, but a consummate con-artist.

The current gang of robber barons is methodically dismantling our historic democratic traditions so that they can continue with their goal of consolidating control over the rest of the world by establishing a militarist, imperial empire.

Why do the American people allow this? Why do they stand for the Iraq war, that's been going on for more than six years, when everybody knows it was a calamitous mistake to begin with? The same thing can be said for Afghanistan and the new incursions into Pakistan.

Why do they stand for the farce called "health care reform" that's currently consuming the mass media?

Because they've been divided and conquered, that's why.

The oligarchy controls the mass media and public education; all means of communication and transfers of information.

Single payer universal health insurance is a good example.

Can't Americans of every stripe see it as a great program for their betterment?

No. they can't. Those two words, "single payer" are *verboten*! Rarely do you see them in print or hear them spoken in the mass media.

The massive propaganda assault demonizing "single payer" and "public option" is unrelenting. The health insurance and pharmaceutical industries are making billions of dollars on your health. One-third of every health care dollar spent goes into their pockets. And they're not going to give that up without a fight to the death. They're a strong force in the capitalist oligarchy that runs this country.

The people had better come out of their somnambulant state before it's too late.

President Obama promised the closing of Guantánamo, than reversed himself, as he did on many of his other promises. However, he is continuing the construction of detention camps within the United States begun during the Clinton era and before.

Rex 84, short for *Readiness Exercise 1984*, is a plan by the United States federal government to test their ability to detain large numbers of refugees or American citizens in case of civil unrest or national emergency.

Through Rex-84 an undisclosed number of concentration camps were set in operation throughout the United States, for internment of dissidents and others potentially harmful to the state.

Halliburton's subsidiary, KBR, has been raking in a whopping three hundred and eighty-six million dollars for providing these detention and processing capabilities.

The grip of the financial mafia over American society must be broken. The power structure must be placed under the ownership and democratic control of the American people as a whole. The resources plundered by the contemporary robber barons must be taken back and used for social needs.

It's wake up time. The holocaust can come again. This is for real!

Solidarity Forever

Whataya know! A labor leader peeped out from under a rock where he'd been hiding and appeared on television!

It was Richard L. Trumka, Secretary-Treasurer of the AFl-CIO and he pledged his support for the public option in the health care reform proposals currently being debated in Congress. He said he was drawing a line in the sand. I guess he meant that the AFL-CIO would switch its support to the Republicans if the Democrats didn't pass a bill that included a public option.

I haven't seen a labor leader on TV since Jimmy Hoffa disappeared.

Trumka is likely to succeed John J. Sweeney as AFL-CIO president at the forthcoming 2009 convention in September.

When corporate America off-shored its manufacturing plants and out-sourced its best paying jobs, it also sent American labor leaders into hiding.

Union membership in the private sector had fallen to under 9% -- levels not seen since 1932.

Union-busting, running "anti-union" campaigns, employing "union avoidance" consultants, and engaging in unfair labor practices, like firing workers who support their union (which is illegal) have contributed to this decline in membership.

For all its history, the assault on labor has been overwhelming, continuous, inhuman and destructive from the beginning of the industrial revolution to this very day.

Labor leaders have been coerced, co-opted, or corrupted; they've been framed, jailed or neutralized in some way. Only when capitalism is in the throes of crisis, deep depression, and near collapse can labor leaders like Eugene V. Debs and John L Lewis emerge.

Debs organized the American Railway Union in 1893, became a confirmed Socialist while serving time in prison for refusing to comply with a federal court injunction, ran for President four times on the Socialist Party ticket, the last time from prison in 1920 and received nearly a million votes.

John L. Lewis led the United Mine Workers in organizing most of the coal industry, was one of the organizers of the Congress of Industrial Organizations (CIO) in 1936 and joined the Reuther brothers, Walter and Victor, in organizing the United Auto Workers' sit-in strikes against General Motors at their Flint, Michigan plants.

For forty-four bitterly cold winter days the auto workers in Flint held out, eventually inspiring more than two-thirds of General Motors 145 thousand other production workers to strike as well, at dozens of other plants. The strikers in Flint seized, shut down, and occupied one, than two, and then three of the key GM plants. Suddenly, workers everywhere were sitting down. There were 477 sit-down strikes by the end of 1937, involving more than half a million workers.

It was a stunning victory for the United Auto Workers. It led the way—and swiftly—to the unionization of workers throughout heavy industry and, ultimately, to unionization in all fields.

The National Labor Relations Act, known as the Wagner Act, introduced by Senator Robert Wagner of New York and signed into law by President Franklin Roosevelt in 1935, was supposed to end the assault on labor and guaranteed the rights of labor to organize, engage in collective bargaining, and take part in strikes and other forms of concerted activity in support of their demands.

But what happened?

Not much. Those days will never come back. Corporate America found other ways to destroy the labor movement.

Although the Wagner Act is still on the books, it's just a monument to earlier times.

But the class struggle persists into the 21st Century.

The current recession progresses—unemployment rising, foreclosures mounting, credit cards failing. Tent cities proliferate around the country, a prelude to the new Hoovervilles.

Militancy will grow out of desperation and workers will begin to fight to change the system when "they have nothing to lose but their chains," as an old analyst of capitalism once said.

Liberals and progressives thought they would be spared all this when Barack Obama made his entrance on a black charger. Even the hardiest of the wishful thinkers are now having the scales falling from their eyes.

"On virtually every issue of importance, President Obama has sided with corporate interests and the wealthy," says Dave Lindorff in Counterpunch. (8/20/09)

"He has taken the concept of selling out to corporate interests and compromising with Republicans to such remarkable heights that progressives hopefully can no longer be confused about the irretrievably corrupted nature of the Democratic Party."

"Health care reform has become a sad joke… instead of taking on the insurance industry, the hospital companies and the pharmaceutical industry and other parts of the profit-making medical-industrial complex, Obama cut deals with all of them behind closed doors, assuring that their profits would be left untouched …"

Isn't it about time labor leaders started showing up again?

They better because the current recession which is slouching toward depression of the 1933 variety needs them more than ever.

Workers, today, can't afford to buy the goods they make. There's no purchasing power around and it is purchasing power that will stop the slide to oblivion.

Only a strong labor movement can save capitalism from itself, again.

Fight Back:
Revoke Insurance Company Charters

We have the mechanism—built into our system—to save our country.

Every corporation or limited liability company in the United States is chartered by a state.

A corporate charter is a document filed with a US state by the founders of a corporation detailing the major components of a company such as its objectives, its structure and its planned operations. If the charter is approved by the state government, the company becomes a legal corporation.

Health insurance companies are such legal corporations with state charters.

David Korten, author of *"When Corporations Rule the World"*, points out that "the basic design of the private-benefit corporation was created in 1600 when the British crown chartered the British East India Company as what is best described as a legalized criminal syndicate to colonize the resources and economies of distant lands..."

Today's American corporations evolved from that.

The corporation is a separate legal entity having its own rights, privileges, and liabilities distinct from those of its members. The private-benefit corporation is just that—a corporation chartered for its own private benefit, but it has to provide some socially positive good. If the corporation, chartered by the state, fails to provide the function for which it is chartered, or misapplies the function, the charter can be revoked. The state giveth and the state can taketh away.

Over the years, the Supreme Court has bestowed additional blessings on corporations. In effect, it has made them almost human, granting them some of the same rights as US citizens, freedom of speech and freedom of the press, for example.

Corporations can express their opinions in public and in the media as you or I can. This gives them enormous power. They can buy up commercial television time and print media ads and faux news coverage because they have the power and the money.

As Sarah Stodola says in *The Brooklyn Rail*, "The Supreme Court has interpreted the constitution in a manner that has allowed corporations to ascend to unprecedented levels of power. The phenomenon even has a name, and that name is 'corporate personhood.' And corporate personhood, friends, is why corporations are able to buy elections."

There is a myriad of different, and overlapping, health care organizations generating a blizzard of paperwork in an administrative wilderness creating enormous waste—thousands, if not millions of people pushing paper around—forms needed to be completed in order to get paid, to say nothing of patients fighting their way through a jungle of obstacles trying to get the health care they need.

In the current situation—in the battle for health care reform—the health insurance industry is exercising its clout. They are spending whopping amounts of money in the mainstream media propagandizing against the health care reform plans being worked on in Congress.

The insurance companies are terrorized by the possibility of a "public option" being included in the bill that comes out of the legislature. Single payer, universal health care is, of course, off the table. Any kind of government plan similar to Medicare, they fear, would jeopardize their billions in health care profits.

Their fear is so great, they are losing their cool. In addition to the propaganda barrage, they are calling out the goon squads to disrupt civil discussion of the various health care reform plans being considered.

Members of Congress and the Senate, who have returned to their constituencies during the August break, and are holding town hall public meetings with their voters to discuss the health care plans are getting a taste of some poisonous medicine.

In addition to angry shouting and disruption, some legislators favoring liberal features in the plan are getting death threats, one even hung is effigy. One goon came to a town meeting with his gun showing.

The insurance companies' misinformation campaign raises the bug-a-boo of "socialized medicine". You'd think it was some kind of torture instead of the government's granting a benefit to the people, very much like Social Security and Medicare.

Some of the behavior the insurance companies are exhibiting, moreover encouraging, is in obvious violation of their charters.

So why isn't something done about it?

Revoke their charters!

Health insurance companies are useless, anyway. They make a profit, and an enormous one, on your health and mine.

End the merry-go-round on health care by political candidates. Get rid of the blood-sucking health insurance industry, once and for all.

There are legitimate grounds on which to revoke their charters!

Make health care for our citizens a right and not a privilege. Small businesses that have the burden of supplying health coverage for their employees will thank us for it. Let's join the world of civilized, industrial nations that provide single payer, universal health insurance for their people. Everybody in. Nobody out.

With the misinformation dispelled, any candidate running for office will get elected on that platform.

Suicide Squad

It's out in the open now. They can't work us over anymore. We know who they are.

Our own oligarchy is out to get us. Global capitalism, feeling the pulse of socialism, is fighting to make the world safe for corporate hegemony—and corporate America is leading the pack.

It began with the destruction of our manufacturing base; off-shoring plants, outsourcing jobs to the lowest wage areas—a race to the bottom.

Will we let them continue the process? Who do we have to stop?

--the military-industrial complex that President Ike Eisenhower warned us about way back in the 20th Century. You can add the mainstream media complex to that…

--and the mighty corporate insurance and pharmaceutical industry that's been keeping proper health care from the American people for over sixty years. When they hear the words "single payer", they reach for their guns.

--and there is the rest of corporate America and its rabble of sycophants, the military contractors and their mercenaries to keep the wars going, the hordes of lobbyists, the propagandists that pervade our institutions, all of academia from grade schools to universities, radio, television, internet, print and new media.

Leading this parade is the custom made front man—POTUS—the President of the United States. It was originally conceived to be a front woman, Hillary Clinton. But along came a Chicagoan, Barack Obama, with a liberal and wishful thinker following, promising to end the wars and give the people single payer health care. He didn't mean any of it but the oligarchy saw a capable con-artist.

So the power structure dumped Hillary and gave the prize to Obama. (Oh, you thought the election had something to do with it?)

Obama fit the image of the POTUS they wanted, from his charm to the color of his skin —the Pied Piper of the South Side—his subservience guaranteed by the two major pillars of the oligarchy. He was quick to assume the "white man's burden".

Hillary, of course, was pissed but she wasn't going to break ranks. She gracefully accepted the position of Secretary of State.

The oligarchy's strategy, the Ayn Rand sagacity of the 20th Century— attack "big" government, return to laissez-faire capitalism.

It goes with monopoly and war. One or two or more wars must be kept going for the economy's sake. Empire building is part of this game. Our empire is extensive.

"Obama is commander-in-chief of an unprecedented network of military bases that is still expanding," says Catherine Lutz in "The New Statesman" (7/30/09). She has made the count. "The global reach of the US military today is unprecedented and unparalleled. Officially, more than 190,000 troops and 115,000 civilian employees are massed in approximately 900 military facilities in 46 countries and territories. The US military owns or rents 795,000 acres of land, with 26,000 buildings and structures, valued at $146bn (£89bn). The bases bristle with an inventory of weapons whose worth is measured in the trillions and whose killing power could wipe out all life on earth several times over."

Obama continues the surge of US troops into Afghanistan. Apparently, he hasn't heard yet that Afghanistan is the graveyard of empires. Hasn't he read Rudyard Kipling?

> "When you're wounded and left on Afghanistan's plains,
> And the women come out to cut up what remains,
> Jest roll to your rifle an' blow out your brains
> An' go to your Gawd like a soldier.

I guess Barack has never kippled.

Obama continues to spread the beneficence of America into what is now called Af-Pak, killing civilians indiscriminately in Pakistan with his new toy, the remote controlled drone.

While all this is going on, we are also leading this country and the world into an economic mess. Employment is flopping, businesses are flipping and home mortgages failing.

Wall Street is being led by the same people who brought it to the ragged edge of disaster. Two of them, Gaithner and Summers, are rewarded by Obama, the former, made Secretary of the Treasury, the latter, top economic advisor to the President.

Legislation for the people is languishing in Congress.

"We have a system today that works well for the insurance industry, but it doesn't always work well for you," President Obama admitted in a speech to a town hall meeting in Raleigh, NC, last week, "what we will have when we pass these reforms, are health insurance consumer protections to make sure that those who have insurance are treated fairly and insurance companies are held accountable."

What he hasn't insisted on is the "public option" in the legislative package. Is he worried he won't have the insurance industry's bundle when he runs for re-election in a few years?

Corporate power stands in the way--antithesis of democracy. Corporate groups are joined together into a single governing body in which the different groups are mandated to negotiate with each other to establish policies in the interest of the multiple groups. This is defined by Wikipedia, the internet encyclopedia, as Corporatism.

Now that we know what is happening and who the scoundrels are, what are we going to do about it?

Yes, Say the Word

Single Payer –National Health Insurance. Horrors! We can't have that! That's Socialism!

Yes, say the word –Socialism!

We can say it and we can have it—at least a little bit of it; even in a capitalist country. A little government for the people—not the corporations—might be a good thing.

Insurance is defined as a promise of compensation for future losses in exchange for a periodic payment. We've been sold every kind there is—life insurance, fire insurance, auto insurance, health insurance…

Health doesn't belong in that group. You can't put a price on a person's health. Health care is a right, like education, and not a privilege.

Insurance Companies are in business for profit. Health insurance companies are in business to make a profit on your health. There should be a law against that!

The health insurance companies, in this country, have made so many billions of dollars on peoples' health, have created so powerful a lobby, bought up so many legislators, it's going to be a mammoth job to get rid of them, but that's what we have to do. Health insurance companies are useless and unnecessary. They're just blood suckers.

Meanwhile their minions, and that includes President Barack Obama, are trying to put on a show. There's a lot of palaver about health care "reform". "Cut health care costs" is the mantra. Have the American people fallen to the level where they will believe that drivel?

It's a red herring. Billions can be saved by getting rid of the health insurance companies. It can be done with the stroke of a pen. But that's the chippie. The purpose of the desperate obfuscation is to save the health insurance industry's sacred profits.

Going in the wrong direction, Obama is gunning for cuts in Medicare and Medicaid? Why pick on the old and the poor, for God's sake!

To use an aphorism of your professed role model, Abraham Lincoln, you're trying to fool all of the people all of the time.

Why do the minions of the health insurance companies cringe when they hear the term "single payer"? Because they know it means real universal health care, the kind civilized, industrial nations, around the world, offer to their citizens.

The health insurance companies (we'll call them bloodsuckers) won't allow the term "single payer" or the term "public option" to be used in the so-called debate that's going on now in the halls of Congress.

Senator Max Baucus, Democrat from Montana, is chairman of the Senate Finance Committee, one of the committees whose job it is to craft some legislation performing the miracle of "health care reform". Recently, in the course of one of these debates, he threw some advocates of the single payer system out of his office. And furthermore, they were arrested! And they happened to be some prominent people in the health care field.

Psychiatrist Carol Paris, one of "the Baucus 13" who got arrested, told The Billings (Montana) Gazette, "The next 60 days are critical; we need to keep the heat on Sen. Baucus (and Congress and the president)."

In an interview with The Gazette, Paris said she used to believe that the private health insurance market could be reformed to improve health care, and she spent several years lobbying for it.

"After a few years, I came to the conclusion that it was just a phenomenal waste of time," she said. "At that point, I just said, there has to be a better place for me to put my time and energy."

Paris is now a member of Physicians for a National Health Program, whose 16,000 members are pushing for a national, publicly funded insurance plan that would replace private health insurance.

When she joined PNHP, to push for a single-payer system, Paris and other members found themselves basically ignored by Congress. They felt they had to do something dramatic to gain attention.

The Billing Gazette reports that they deliberately planned to protest - and get arrested - at a Senate Finance Committee hearing on health reform, chaired by Baucus.

Paris and her colleagues showed up the morning of May 5, spread themselves around in the gallery audience and, one by one, interrupted Baucus as he started the meeting.

"I interrupt this so-called public hearing to bring you the following unpaid political announcement: Put single-payer on the table," Paris said before she was arrested. "My name is Dr. Carol Paris, and I approved this message."

Capitol police arrested the protesters, who have been charged with disrupting Congress.

Amy Goodman of "Democracy Now!" reports that Senator Baucus has received more campaign money from health and insurance industry interests than any other member of Congress. "In the past six years, nearly one-fourth of every dime raised by Baucus and his political-action committee has come from groups and individuals associated with drug companies.

Dr. Paris said her experience in private practice has convinced her that true reform can happen only if private health insurance is replaced with national, public insurance for all.

"No longer would physicians' staff have to spend hours dealing with multiple insurers on billing, and no longer would patients have to worry about which doctor they can go to," she said. "You can go to any doctor of their choice. It's in the private insurance industry where choice is restricted."

Dr. Paris says she hears "over and over and over again" how people are frustrated by the current system, and that as soon as they understand how single-payer would work, they usually support it.

"I think that the only thing that keeps this from happening is the lack of political will by the president and our Congress,"

So, yes, say the word.

A little bit of Socialism, anyone?

Where Were You
When Journalism Died?

The death of Walter Cronkite is an appropriate time to reflect on what's happened to journalism in America.

Walter and I came to CBS around the same time, in the early 1950s. Sig Mickelson, head of the CBS News and Public Affairs division, at the time, brought Walter in to anchor the first television coverage of a presidential election convention in 1952 and incidentally coined the term "anchorman".

Irving Gitlin, who ran the Public Affairs section, under Mickelson, brought me in to produce documentaries. In most cases, network correspondents came out of print journalism, television news producers out of film documentaries. Fred Friendly, who started the controversial program "See It Now" in 1951, came out of radio and always thought of television as radio with pictures, and admitted it.

Cronkite embodied the spirit of television journalism. In the 1960s and 70s, there was still some leeway for experimentation. I produced a number of news documentaries with Walter as host and narrator during that period.

In those days, the networks were still mostly independently owned—they had not yet been conglomerated.

William S. Paley, a cigar-maker in Philadelphia created the Columbia Broadcasting System (CBS) from a small radio network he bought in order to advertise his cigars.

By 1981, when Walter Cronkite handed over the CBS anchor desk to Dan Rather, the process of mergers and acquisitions was well under way.

Television networks were created in order to provide programming to affiliate local stations. The cost of producing the entertainment or news programs was financed through advertising; so commercial operations got into the game from the very beginning. Profits were shared between the network and their affiliated stations.

In the beginning, each network was limited to owning and operating only five local stations, (called the o&os), usually in the major markets, but they serviced many affiliates.

The Federal Communications Commission (FCC), an independent US government agency, established by the Communications Act of 1934, was charged with regulating interstate and international communications by radio, television, wire, satellite and cable. The FCC makes and is supposed to enforce the rules.

Rule #1—the Fairness Doctrine. In news and public affairs programming, stations must present controversial issues of public importance in a manner that is "honest, equitable and balanced" in the Commission's view or they could be subject to losing their broadcast license.

I haven't heard of a case where a station lost its license for this reason, but I guess there must be one. However, in 1987, the FCC abolished the Fairness Doctrine. Oh, well, I guess it didn't matter.

With the coming of color and the cable news networks, television became even more marinated in commercialism than it was when there were only three commercial networks.

As early as 1961, Newton Minnow, then-head of the FCC made his famous "vaste wasteland" speech before the National Association of Broadcasters convention. Minnow gave the broadcasters unshirted hell for not doing more to serve the public interest.

But that message went in one ear and out the other.

As time went on, the FCC kept loosening the reins, allowing the networks more and more latitude, not only in accumulating more and more o&os, but in deregulating mergers and acquisitions as well.

Today, the mainstream media is in a sorry state. Six corporate media giants with a stranglehold on information, control most of what we see, hear, and read. The five largest are AOL Time-Warner; the Walt Disney Company that now owns the ABC Television Network; Bertelsmann, a German firm with more than $15 billion in media assets; Sumner Redstone's Viacom that owns CBS; Rupert Murdoch's News Corporation that controls and runs Fox News on TV and the New York Post on paper and all the news they fix to print.

In addition, they all have interests in major movie studios, other TV channels and networks, cable companies, most of the music companies, book publishing, retail stores, amusement parks, video games, and merchandising and on and on.

Such a concentration of media power in so few hands violates every known theory of a free market place of ideas that is the essence of democracy.

"While television is supposed to be free," said Walter Lippmann, prominent journalist, in 1959, "it has, in fact, become the creature, the servant and indeed the prostitute of merchandising."

Despite his distain for commercial television, Lippmann also exhibited his distain for the intelligence of the American public. He didn't think they were smart enough to understand complex political issues. The public needed journalists to filter the news for them; elites to interpret what policy-makers and politicians were doing, something called "manufacturing consent" as defined by Edward S. Herman and Noam Chomsky in their book by that name, subtitled "The Political Economy of the Mass Media".

In their view, the media serves and propagandizes for "powerful societal interests" that controls and finances them. These interests have important agendas that they want to advance and they have the means with which to do it. It is not accomplished by crude intervention but by the "selection of right-thinking personnel, by editors and working journalists who internalize the priorities and definitions of newsworthiness that conform to the institution's policy."

Reporters working in the field call it "Do-It-Yourself Censorship". You have to know just how far you can push the envelope or you won't be working in the field very long.

The big change in television came when news became a profit center. With the collapse of the Fairness Doctrine and the laxity of the FCC, the News Departments at the Networks no longer felt they had to perform a public service. "Earn your own way, Buddy. Get a sponsor. Show a profit." News shows started running commercials.

This was the new media world Walter Cronkite saw coming. He didn't like it, either.

Good-bye, Walter.

Good night and good luck, as Ed Murrow would say.

And that's the way it is.

Convergence

Conspiracy theories never die, they just fade away. There is one that seems to persist. What really happened on 9/11?

The 9/11 Commission Report, released on April 24th 2007, about six years after the events, was about as accurate as the Warren Commission report that supposedly revealed the facts of the Kennedy assassination in 1963.

For those who are not old enough to remember, 9/11 is a euphemism for the date, September 11, 2001, when the events took place.

Isn't it about time the mainstream media or the alternative media or even the Congress started finding out what really happened?

Two thousand nine hundred and four people died in the attacks on the World Trade Center, the two main towers and several of the smaller buildings around them, on the Pentagon and in the crash of the airliner in a field near Shanksville, in rural Pennsylvania.

The Bush Administration immediately attributed these acts of terrorism by hijacked planes to Osama bin Laden, and al-Qaeda, the terrorist organization he is said to lead. The propaganda onslaught was so pervasive; the truth of it has now become conventional wisdom.

No one has ever explained the controlled demolitions that brought down the World Trade towers. There is undeniable evidence. There are plenty of witnesses that heard and saw results of the explosions of planted bombs. It is naïve to think that fires caused by aviation gasoline on upper floors could have collapsed the towers. Any honest structural engineer will verify that.

The Bush Administration responded with a "war on terror", planned long before 9/11, by invading Afghanistan to depose its Taliban government, accused of harboring Osama bin Laden.

It seems reasonable to suspect that some form of collusion, call it conspiracy, took place between parties on both sides of the equation prior to the attacks. One side may have provided the hijackers, others participating in the conspiracy, the training at small, local airports in the United States. A piece of incidental intelligence, that may be meaningful or perhaps, not—Marvin Bush, the president's younger brother, was a principal in a company called Securacom that provided security to the World Trade Center. On several occasions, before the 9/11 attacks, Securacom had the towers evacuated so that "security services" could be provided.

There would have had to be a full-fledged conspiracy for an intricate caper like the planting of explosives to have been pulled off. Don't put anything past this government.

Conspiracy theories about 9/11 are rife. The most prominent one, of course, is the 9/11 Commission Report, the official explanation of the US Government. They left a myriad of unanswered questions that any good "truth" commission would have explored.

Since all 19 of the hijackers of the four planes were recruited through al-Qaeda and most, if not all, were Saudi nationals, wouldn't it be a good idea to look into their connections with the Saudi Arabian government and the ruling elites, one of the closest being the bin Laden family.

We're not implying guilt by association here, but George W Bush, 43, and his family, including his father, Bush, 41, had strong personal and business ties with the Saudi royal family.

President Obama, when he took office, was quick to assert that there would be no investigation of the Bush Administration depredations. Why?

However, last year, the U.S. Congress mandated an investigation of illegal wiretapping by the inspectors general of five federal agencies. Their report, recently released, and as reported by The New York Times (7-11-09) "The Central Intelligence Agency and other intelligence branches viewed the program, which allowed eavesdropping without warrants on the international communications of Americans, "as a useful tool but could not link it directly to counterterrorism successes, presumably arrests or thwarted plots".

Investigative journalist Lucy Komisar, in her new book, "A Game as Old as Empire", examines George W. Bush's startling assertion that there was a link between Saddam Hussein and Osama bin Laden.

She says, "There was a link, but not the one Bush was selling. The link between Hussein and bin Laden was their banker, B.C.C.I. (Bank of Credit and Commerce International) But, the link went beyond the dictator and the jihadist -- it passed through Saudi Arabia and stretched all the way to George W. Bush and his father."

"BCCI was a dirty offshore bank that then-President Ronald Reagan's Central Intelligence Agency used to run guns to Hussein, finance Osama bin Laden, move money in the illegal Iran-Contra operation and carry out other "agency" black ops. The Bushes also benefited privately; one of the bank's largest Saudi investors helped bail out George W. Bush's troubled oil investments."

The 2008 election victory was a time for celebration. Electricity was in the air. With Barack Obama we were going to end the wars, repeal the Patriot Act, restore Habeus Corpus. Make our nation whole again. Many of our youth joined the parade of the Wishful Thinkers.

Disillusionment set in very fast. No end to the wars. On the contrary, a shift of forces from one war to another, the start of a third. No single payer health plan. No end to warrantless searches. No closing of Gitmo. No Habeus Corpus. The list goes on. A continuation of the Bush policies and even better.

One hapless blogger, Ted Rall on The Smirking Chimp moans, "I haven't forgiven George W. Bush for stealing two elections, starting two wars, bankrupting the treasury and doing his damnedest to turn the U.S. into a fascist state. He deserves one of hell's hottest picnic spots…the worst president the U.S. had ever had—until this one. I don't care about window dressing. Sure, it's nice that Obama is intelligent. But policies matter--not charm. And Obama's policies are at least as bad as Bush's."

Major historical changes are takes place, world-wide, and here at home; but we're not supposed to know about them.

Corporatism is trumping nationalism.

Benito Mussolini, pre-World War II dictator of Italy, had a word for it. Fascism. What do you call it?

Chink in the Armor

"I am going to reform health care," says Barack Obama.

"Socialist!" cries the right wing.

When Barack says we've got to "cut health costs", read "cut benefits". He has openly called for "savings" in Medicare, Medicaid and Social Security.

What a socialist!

He isn't even talking about single-payer universal health care, the standard for most civilized, industrial, "capitalist" countries.

Obama doesn't dare lay a finger on America's iron-clad health insurance industry that gave him millions for his election campaign— an industry that is completely useless, eats 33% of health dollars for bureaucratic overhead and profits and contributes nothing to your health. Medicare does a lot more for the elderly with only about 3% for administration.

Where is the change we can believe in?

Socialism seems to be the buzz-word of the day. You see the word in the news now, quite frequently, when previously its use was judged to be unseemly. Maybe that's a step forward.

"We Are All Socialists Now!" shouts the front page on Newsweek Magazine (3-28-09).

The cry is picked up by the mainstream media.

Wikipedia defines socialism as "public or state ownership and administration of the means of production and distribution of goods, and a society characterized by equality for all individuals, with a fair or egalitarian method of compensation."

Sounds reasonable.

Of course, its roots are grounded in the analysis of capitalism by Karl Marx in the second half of the 19th Century. He believed that capitalism is based on the exploitation of the working class by the bourgeoisie and profit is derived from surplus value created by the worker in the process of production. Marx argued that capitalism, like previous socioeconomic systems, will produce internal tensions—contradictions—which will eventually lead to its destruction.

In capitalism, improvements in technology and rising levels of productivity leads to the paradox, characteristic of crises in capitalism, of "poverty in the midst of plenty," or more precisely, crises of overproduction in the midst of under-consumption.

Just as capitalism replaced feudalism, socialism will in its turn replace capitalism and open the way to a classless society.

The Rasmussen Reports, a polling service highly regarded for accuracy, recently found that only 53% of American adults believe that capitalism is better than socialism.

Adults under 30 are essentially evenly divided: 37% prefer capitalism, 33% socialism, and 30% are undecided.

There is a partisan gap as well. Republicans—by an 11-to-1 margin—favor capitalism. Democrats are much more closely divided: Just 39% say capitalism is better while 30% prefer socialism.

The standard argument of the anti-socialist partisans is that socialism doesn't work. Someone must have put out a group-think talking point list. You hear the same arguments in the same words coming from all directions.

The antagonists always point to the failure of the Soviet Union. Surely, it was a failure, but it wasn't socialism. In the first few years after the Russian Revolution, the Bolsheviks floundered around. The country was in a state of chaos. On Lenin's death in 1924, Stalin seized power and made himself dictator. End of socialism before it began.

These changes in socio-economic systems must be viewed in the long sweep of history. After all, there were only three of them—primitive communism, feudalism and capitalism. Give the world a break. These things take time. Capitalism floundered for about two hundred years with its wars and booms and busts, and its destruction of the environment and is only now reaching its tipping point.

The contention of the naysayers is that human greed has to be factored into a socio-economic system. However, after two centuries of laissez-faire capitalism and unrestrained human greed, they had to leash the beast. They put restraints on the system.

Then the battle of deregulation began anew and the deregulators won. They brought the world capitalist system to the current crisis and the point of economic collapse. Now we're hearing talk of socialism.

Right now we're in a state of near paralysis. Obama is even having trouble getting Republican support for his stimulus package. Meanwhile unemployment is growing by 600,000 or more per month and foreclosures on the American dream continue.

Where will this end up? Do you see a Hooverville in your future?

Or are we going to take some action in a positive, socialist direction before capitalism self-destructs?

Being an eternal optimist, I see demonstrations and Gandhi type civil disobedience in the not too distant future to put the heat on Obama to fulfill some of his promises.

Obama may be a hard nut to crack. It was the young and liberal that flocked to his side, an important part of his base that put him in the White House, but the signs were there that he was the oligarch's boy early in the game.

So, instead of his being our knight on the white charger, we're going to have the put the screws to him to get him to behave. No small task. Can we do it?

Where Is Obama Taking Us?

Does Barack Obama think he can stop the collapse of an economic system by throwing money at it? That's what he's doing in massive amounts, in stimulus packages, budgets and bailouts, and it's our money.

It seems to be having little effect. With job losses at the rate of 600,000 per month, 660,000 last month, the economy is slip-slidin' toward a 1930s type depression.

The official unemployment rate is now 8.5% but, according to economist Peter Morici at the University of Maryland, the real unemployment rate is closer to 17% when discouraged adults who have left the labor force and part-time workers are factored in.

A total of 5.1 million jobs have gone AWOL since December 2007.

After the public outrage generated by the AIG bailout and bonus give-a-way, a rational human being would think the administration wouldn't let it happen again, but it has. Fannie Mae and Freddie Mac, the quasi-government mortgage providers, who had two heavy hands in creating the crisis, are now giving themselves bonuses, too.

According to The Wall Street Journal, 7,600 employees will be getting $210 million in "retention" bonuses for their incompetence. The maximum retention bonus for any individual executive will be $1.5 million.

Any wonder capitalism is having heart failure?

With the economy in this fatal condition, the banks tottering, the auto industry on the ropes, financial disclosures, this week, reveal to what extent the Obama Administration is a tool of Wall Street.

Obama has no compunctions about using taxpayer money to buy up toxic assets and taking the heat off hedge funds.

The Administration's Auto Task Force, rejecting the recovery plans of Chrysler and General Motors, has put heightened pressure on the industry to hammer the auto workers union, force brutal cuts on wages, benefits and pensions.

Even more scurrilous are Obama's repeated assurances to Wall Street that he will slash social spending, including Medicare, Medicaid and Social Security.

It's out in the open, now—they can't work us over anymore— top Obama advisors directly involved in setting these policies, have received millions from Wall Street firms, including those that have received huge taxpayer bailouts.

Lawrence Summers, Obama's top economic advisor, a glaring example, pocketed $5 million as a managing director of D.E. Shaw, one of the biggest hedge funds in the world, and another $2.7 million for speeches delivered to Wall Street firms that have received government bailout money. This includes $45,000 from Citigroup and $67,500 each from JPMorgan Chase and the now-liquidated Lehman Brothers. Last year, Summers walked away with $135,000 for a speech to Goldman Sachs executives.

The New York Times noted Saturday (4-4-09) "Mr. Summers, the director of the National Economic Council, wields important influence over Mr. Obama's policy decisions for the troubled financial industry, including firms from which he recently received payments."

Any conflict of interest here?

It's no secret that Summers was a leading advocate of banking deregulation. The *Times* article notes that among his current responsibilities is deciding "whether—and how—to tighten regulation of hedge funds."

Summers is not an exception. He's typical of the Wall Street insiders who make up the White House team, filled with multi-millionaires, presided over by a president who parlayed his own political career into a multi-million-dollar fortune, according to investigative reporter, Tom Eley.

There is Michael Froman, deputy national security adviser for international economic affairs, who worked for Citigroup and received more than $7.4 million from the bank from January of 2008 until he entered the Obama administration this year. This included a $2.25 million year-end bonus handed him this past January, within weeks of his joining the Obama administration. Citigroup has thus far been the beneficiary of $45 billion in cash and over $300 billion in government guarantees of its bad debts. Can this be called "quid pro quo"?

David Axelrod, senior adviser to the president, was paid $1.55 million last year from two consulting firms he controls. He has agreed to buyouts that will garner him another $3 million over the next five years. His disclosure claims personal assets of between $7 and $10 million.

Obama's deputy national security adviser, Thomas E. Donilon, was paid $3.9 million by a Washington law firm whose major clients include Citigroup, Goldman Sachs and the private equity firm Apollo Management.

Donilon worked as Executive Vice President for Law and Policy at Fannie Mae. The Washington Times reported that Donilon made millions for work that included supervising Fannie Mae's lobbying against increased regulation. [

Another member of the gang, Louis Caldera, director of the White House Military Office, made $227,155 last year from IndyMac Bancorp, the California bank that heavily promoted subprime mortgages. It collapsed last summer and was placed under federal receivership.

And that's not all.

Multi-millionaire Wall Street insiders populate second and third-tier positions in the Obama administration as well.

David Stevens, tapped by Obama to head the Federal Housing Administration, is the president of a real estate brokerage firm. From 1999 to 2005 Stevens served as a top executive for Freddie Mac.

Neal Wolin, Obama's deputy counsel for economic policy, is a top executive at the insurance giant Hartford Financial Services, where his salary was $4.5 million.

The story goes on…

Are you shocked—shocked!

A parallel set of characters can be found in the war, excuse me, defense department, lined up in the cabinet.

Remember "Change you can believe in!"

From the start, Obama played the populist, critic of the war in Iraq and won over a youth and liberal base, all the while being backed by the oligarchy with massive campaign funds.

So, where are you going to take us with this gang of hundreds, Mr. Obama?

It's Wake-Up Time

We don't have nightmares asleep any more—we wake up into them.

An endless war. An imminent crash. An election campaign in which the three contenders are corporate candidates. High crimes and misdemeanors that go unchallenged.

The perfect storm.

This is the United States where the America Dream, at one time, could become a reality. This is the America of Franklin Roosevelt who built a safety net under his people. This is the America of Watergate that forced accountability on its leaders.

No more. We've wakened from the dream into a nightmare.

The Iraq war must go on, says John McCain, Republican presidential candidate, who thinks it will take a hundred years to achieve victory. No one has yet come up with a definition of victory. Democratic candidates talk about ending the war with a variety of timetables that everybody knows will never happen. Big Oil calls the shots.

We're all getting along just fine with the war as a background hum, so why rock the boat? The anti-war movement of 2003, that seemed so promising at the time, has evaporated into a feel-good miasma.

There is no draft. Your son or daughter will not be affected. They'll probably go on to college. It's only those invisibles down there, America's new underclass that provides the cannon fodder. So why bother? The corporate owned mainstream media has joined the parade with colors and lies flying, eating out your brain. The hype of the "surge" has become a dirge. Better wear that lapel flag pin to prove you're patriotic!

Everyone is waiting for that other shoe to drop. The Bush-Cheney gang is down to its last nine months. In January of 2009, something new happens.

It's a long wait. The joisting has been going on for almost a year.

While Barack Obama is a favorite boy of Wall Street, Hillary not only does well on the "street", but is also the darling of the defense (war) industry. Obama picked up a respectable $474,428 from Wall Street's Goldman Sachs as well as anywhere from a quarter million or more from Time Warner, Citigroup, Inc, Lehman Brothers, JP Morgan Chase & Co among others.

Hillary did better with Lockheed Martin, Boeing, Northrop-Grumman, Raytheon, and General Dynamics who gave Democratic candidates $103,900, Hillary getting the lion's share of that.

According to the Federal Election Commission, Republican John McCain raked in a whopping $58,950,601 as of March 1st, $684,294 of it coming from PACs.

The oligarchy always hedges its bets. One way or the other, it gets the man (or woman) it wants.

Meanwhile, George W. Bush, whose rating are in the gutter, continues to decimate this country with impunity. While Dick Cheney is on a fishing trip to Iraq, baiting the waters for an attack on Iran, Bush continues to tweak Ahmadinejad. The two war criminals are trying to squeeze another war into their repertoire before they leave a desecrated stage of history in January of 2009. One war isn't enough. Or is this just another "wag the dog" strategy; a political move to get Republican John McCain elected—your Commander-in-Chief for the hundred years war…?

Wars are usually started to pull the economy out of recession. With Iraq, we have a recession and a war going on at the same time. As Ike warned, beware the military-industrial complex. Now we have a military-industrial-contractor complex.

Notwithstanding the 160,000, or so, US military troops in Iraq, there are about 180,000 private contractors, including up to 50,000 employed in military functions. Blackwater, the leading mercenary contractor, has made deals with both the State and the Defense Departments. When top brass come to visit, it's the Blackwater mercenaries that protect them. Apparently, they don't trust our American troops; another good reason for them to go home pouting.

There is a world economic collapse in the making and the US is in the eye of the storm. The Fed inflates the money supply to stave off recession which drives prices up as wages fall due to the off-shoring of our manufacturing plants.

You can count on this government to do the wrong thing. The Bush administration gives tax cuts to the rich when they should be soaking them, as Roosevelt did to help the nation climb out of the last depression. What we need is a new New Deal, putting people to work rebuilding the infrastructure of the country, instead of a stimulus package handing out $600 checks. The money will mostly be used by debt-loaded Americans for paying off overdue credit cards. No shot in the arm for the economy there.

Our two-party system is broken. That will become evident at the Democrat's Denver convention, in August, when a choice has to be made between their squabbling candidates, Billary and Obama. Early primaries were a disaster. Enmities have hardened after months of cloying, boring debates. If super-delegates have to be used to decide on a candidate, the Democratic Party might as well fold its big tent and disappear into the night.

The beginning of another bad dream?

Two Degrees of Separation

In the beginning was the word and the word was with God and the word was God.

"Let there be light: and there was light"

It was Karl Marx and Friedrich Engels who taught us about the Class Struggle—the inexorable clash between the bourgeoisie and the proletariat.

"The history of all hitherto existing society is the history of class struggle" said Marx and Engels in The Communist Manifesto. (1848)

By the time this famous duo arrived on the scene, the industrial revolution in England was humming right along and the young entrepreneurs needed cotton for their cotton gins and wool for their weaving looms.

They got the cotton from the plantations in their colonies on the North American continent and in the Caribbean. They got their wool by passing the Enclosure Acts, in England, throwing the small farmers off the common lands, enclosing them and raising sheep.

The triangular slave trade was characteristic of it all. It operated for two and a half centuries, the 17th, 18th and part of the 19th, carrying slaves, cash crops and manufactured goods between West Africa, the Caribbean, the American colonies and the European colonial powers.

The trade in human cargo was lucrative; slave labor on the plantation even more so. Slavers owned all of the slaves' labor power.

But life on the plantation was not all sweetness and light. Class struggle seethed beneath the repression. There were slave revolts, murders, slow-downs and sabotage. Run-a-way slaves were a nagging problem. Aided by the abolitionists, a network of underground railroads, routes of escape, were extended.

Meanwhile, feudalism was emerging from the middle ages.

The nobles had been given huge swatches of land by the monarchies. The serfs worked the land. A system of lord and vassal emerged, with the lord taking everything the serf produced leaving him only enough to survive and to reproduce himself. Later, in the United States, they called it share-cropping.

It was another stage in the class struggle, albeit, a small one—from slave to serf—where the serf got a little more than the slave.

Eric Hobsbawm, a British historian, says the Industrial Revolution "broke out" in the 1780s but other historians have argued that it wasn't a "revolution" at all but more evolutionary since the process of economic and social change took place gradually. It was a period in which capitalism reared its ugly head.

Excuse me for saying that, but it's been capitalism that has brought us to the point where our planet might not be able to take much more of it.

Industrial activity steals from the vitality of the earth's biosphere.

The earth's finite resources should be managed so that the human race and the rest of the organisms on earth can survive. But capitalist enterprise is concerned primarily with present and future profits and is constantly under pressure to maximize them.

It doesn't take into account the fact that the economy relies on the environment.

Furthermore, the capitalist system, as the slave system and the feudal system, is based on theft—theft of the worker's labor power.

The capitalist makes his profit by extracting the surplus value created by the worker in the process of production. The worker's struggle is measured by how much of the value of his labor power he can keep in the form of wages. Through labor unions, strikes, collective bargaining, and other forms of struggle, the worker fights to claim what's rightfully his.

An organized labor force with some political clout, at times, has given capitalism some viability by maintaining a more equitable distribution of wealth, but when capital wins the ball game, the wealth is siphoned right to the top.

Capitalism, right now, is in a world economic crisis, a condition not seen since the 1930s.

Heads of states are running around looking for answers and describing symptoms to explain problems. Defaulting loans. Toxic assets. Frozen credit. These are manifestations of the crisis, not the root causes.

The propaganda mills picture capitalism as the ***victim of vaguely*** identified villains—reckless speculators, poorly regulated banks, excessively-leveraged hedge funds, greedy and overpaid executives, and even the downtrodden American consumer.

These "explanations" interpret the crisis as the product of various faults and errors, rather than the result of the contradictions within the capitalist system.

Establishment economists are blind to the contradictions. They adopt an apologetic attitude toward capitalism which denies the existence of economic contradictions that lead to crisis and breakdown.

Marx can tell them the cause of the current crisis: "Crises exist because these contradictions exist...."

When will we get real and start questioning capitalism itself? The profit system. The free market. The invisible hand?

There are two degrees of separation between the slave system and capitalism. What will the third one be—and when will it come?

Coxey's Army Will March Again!

⌣⁊⌒

After the Panic of 1893, the worst gut-wrenching economic depression in US history to that time, Jacob Coxey, an Ohio populist, organized the first march on Washington by unemployed workers to lobby the government to create jobs by building roads and public works.

Sound familiar?

The march originated with 100 men in Massillon, Ohio, passed through Pittsburgh, Becks Run and Homestead, Pennsylvania picking up marchers on the way. Various groups from around the country joined the march. Many of these protesters were unemployed railroad workers.

William Hogan, a railroad worker, and some of his followers commandeered a Northern Pacific Railway train for their trek to Washington. They fought off federal marshals but were eventually stopped by federal troops.

Fifteen hundred troops were stationed in Washington to meet the marchers, and thousands more available in anticipation of further trouble.

Coxey's Army of five hundred weary marchers made it to Washington on April 30, 1894.

Coxey and other leaders of the movement were arrested the next day for walking on the grass of the United States Capitol. That was the upshot. A bit of an anti-climax.

But it was the first significant protest march on Washington, in a long history of marches, and the origin of the expression, "Enough food to feed Coxey's Army".

The next big one—the veterans' Bonus March of 1932—the self-proclaimed Bonus Expeditionary Force of some 43,000 marchers, composed of 17,000 World War I veterans, their families and affiliated groups hit the road to the nation's capitol.

In the depth of The Great Depression the veterans were as destitute as just about everyone else.

On discharge from the army, they had been promised a bonus based on their pay in the service plus compound interest. The bonuses were to be redeemable in 1945, but the veterans wanted their money NOW!

Walter W. Waters, a former Army sergeant, led the Bonus Army and hammered Congress for immediate payment. There was some support in Congress for prompt redemption, but President Hoover and most Republicans in Congress opposed it because it would negatively affect the Federal government's budget and depression relief programs.

The 43,000-plus Bonus marchers camping in Washington D.C. left a pretty big muddy footprint. They camped on the grass and lawns between government buildings where Coxey had been arrested. But the treatment they received was much different.

They were driven by federal troops from the capitol grounds, chased across the Anacostia River where they set up a Hooverville in a swampy, muddy area called Anacostia Flats.

Their camps were built from materials scavenged from a nearby rubbish dump. Hoovervilles had been proliferating across the country since the beginning of The Great Depression, named for their President whose flawed policies had brought them on.

In 1930, St. Louis, Missouri, had the largest Hooverville in America. The one in New York City's Central Park existed from 1931 to 1933.

On July 28, 1932, Attorney General Mitchell ordered the evacuation of the veterans from Anacostia Flats. If they resisted, they would be shot. They resisted. Two of them were shot and killed.

President Hoover ordered the U.S. Army to effect the evacuation.

At 4:45 pm, that same day, commanded by Gen Douglas McArthur, the 12th Infantry Regiment and the 3rd Cavalry Regiment, supported by six battle tanks under the command of Maj. George S. Patton (later General of World War II fame), the US Army attacked its own veterans.

After a cavalry charge, infantry, with fixed bayonets and adamsite gas, a riot control agent, entered the Bonus Army camps and successfully evicted veterans, families and camp followers. They set fire to the campsites. Hundreds of veterans were injured, several were killed including William Hushka and Eric Carlson.

Hoover's action outraged the nation and many believe the incident was the cause of his loss to Democrat Franklin D. Roosevelt in the upcoming election.

The Bonus March of 1932 was a landmark of dissent and protest in the United States. Prior to that time, only the Women's Suffrage march on

March 3, 1913 when 5000 marched to support women's voting rights could be compared with it.

After the Bonus March, marches on Washington went rampant.

In the 1960s, there was the March on Washington for Jobs and Freedom at which Dr. Martin Luther King Jr. gave his "I Have a Dream" speech before 250,000 marchers.

From 1965 to 1969 there were eight marches on Washington protesting the Vietnam War, building to the two famous National Mobilizations to End the War—the Vietnam Moratorium at which 200,000 demonstrated on October 15, 1969 and again a month later on November 15, when a striking 600,000 demonstrated against the war in Vietnam.

On April 19, 1971, Vietnam Veterans Against the War organized 2000 veterans to camp on the Mall in Washington while others protested all over the city. It was the day veteran John Kerry testified in front of the Senate, making his feeling known about the war.

There were five other protest marches against the war in the 1970s, one calling for mass action by Vietnam anti-war militants to shut down the federal government.

On April 27, 1974, ten thousand marched on Washington calling for the impeachment of President Richard M. Nixon. Shortly after that he resigned.

In July of 1978, thousands of Native Americans finished their "Longest Walk", a 3200 mile hike from San Francisco to Washington D. C. where they rallied on the Mall for religious freedom for traditional American Indians.

The decade ended with a "tractorcade" on February 5, 1979 when 6000 family farmers drove their tractors to Washington to protest American farm policy and on October 14th when the National March on Washington for Lesbian and Gay Rights took place. The first of its kind, the march drew 100,000 gay men and lesbians to demand equal civil rights.

The 1980s were distinguished by the AFL-CIO organized march of 260,000 unionists to protest the Reagan Administration labor and domestic policies and The Great Peace March for Global Nuclear Disarmament from Los Angeles, California to Washington D. C. to raise awareness of the growing danger of nuclear proliferation and to advocate for complete, verifiable elimination of nuclear weapons from the earth.

On October 11, 1987, a second National March on Washington for Lesbian and Gay Rights took place, this time drawing half a million gay men and women, not only calling for equal civil rights but also demanding government action in the fight against AIDS.

Marches during the 90s were relatively sparse, but they did include a couple of big ones. In the last year of the George Herbert Walker Bush Administration there were Dual Marches against the Gulf War on January 19th and 26th 1991. Their estimated draw was 250,000 and 25,000 respectively. On April 25, 1993, there was a third March on Washington for Lesbian, Gay and Bi Equal Rights. Organizers estimate that one million attended. Then there was the Million Man March on October 16, 1995.

The 21st Century was met with a couple of major protest marches anticipating President George W. Bush's attack on Iraq.

The first of numerous protests against a war with Iraq started on October 26, 2002 by ant-war umbrella groups including United for Peace and Justice and MoveOn.org that drew over 100,000 at the Washington protest, and again on January 18, 2003 when an estimated 200,000 attended.

Nonetheless, Bush attacked Iraq in March of 2003. Saddam Hussein was disposed of rather quickly, but the war dragged on through Bush's interminable eight-year administration and is now in its 6th year and has become Obama's war.

President Obama is now the owner of two wars, Iraq and Afghanistan, (when you break it, you own it, as Colin Powell so aptly put it) and he is not only planning to escalate the Afghan war but is looking forward to starting two more of his own, Pakistan (which he had already robot bombed) and Iran, which he has threatened while staring into the face of an oncoming depression.

When enough Americans lose their homes and their jobs and get thrown out on the street, they will also lose their apathy and start marching again.

Jacob Coxey, here we come!

Treason, Stratagems and Spoils

Capitalism has hit the wall.

We're facing a world-wide economic collapse. Where is Trotsky now that we really need him!

It was Leon Trotsky, an original Bolshevik, who said that socialism (or communism) couldn't succeed in one country. There had to be world revolution.

"Workers of the world unite! You have nothing to lose but your chains."

There was a deep disagreement between Trotsky and V. I. Lenin, a fellow Bolshevik, on this point. Lenin believed that socialism (or communism) could be achieved in one country, Russia, which was in a shambles at the end of World War I.

Lenin prevailed. Tsar Nicholas II was overthrown. The Bolsheviks (majority) defeated the Mensheviks (minority) and Alexander Kerensky (Labour Party) and the Soviet Union was born. But socialism didn't last long. After Lenin's death in 1924, Stalin seized power. He made himself dictator and all the "old Bolsheviks" were tried, convicted and "eliminated" resulting from the rigged treason trials held in the mid-1930s. Trotsky fled. He was found in Mexico with an ax in his head in 1940.

So much for socialism (or communism) in one country.

Now we're confronting a new situation. The entire world is in economic shambles.

Obama now has a stimulus package of $787 billion with which he is trying to re-inflate the economic bubble that just burst. He's trying to put into effect a faux New Deal with a faux WPA, with government taking the reins and repairing the infrastructure with shovel-ready projects to create jobs.

Vladimir Putin, former KGB agent in the Soviet Union, now Prime Minister of a capitalist Russia, warned Obama not to go socialist. That's like telling the Pope not to go Catholic.

Don't listen to Putin, Mr. Obama!

The contradictions of capitalism have come home to roost.

Stop throwing money at all those financial institutions big enough to fail. It's only paper. It will do no good.

Nationalize the banks and keep the banksters from ripping off the taxpayers.

Contradiction Number One, you can't make money with money. You can only create wealth by producing something of real value like food, clothing or shelter.

Money is a medium of exchange, defined in Wikipedia as "an intermediary used in trade to avoid the inconveniences of a pure barter system."

Only God's gifts of nature (the land and everything beneath it and above it) and man's labor can create value or wealth. The gifts of nature should belong to everyone—not a privileged few.

The economic system of the US has been left with paper while the real value and the wealth of this country have taken flight. The captains of industry have off-shored a good part of our manufacturing base, our wealth, to other nations. They are outsourcing skilled labor and they are also using the H-1B visa to allow US employers to bring foreign workers into the United States and employ them at wages US workers couldn't live on.

So our country is hollowed out.

Why have they done this?

The answer is simple. Profits. Move your plants to where labor is cheapest.

But there is always a hitch. Contradiction Number Two. Profits are derived from the surplus value extracted from the worker in the process of production. You need a working class to exploit and the working class must be able to reproduce itself. Yes, you capitalists hate'em but you need'em.

Just about everybody knows about this Marxist theory—certainly workers who are the victims of it and economists who have studied it and societies who live under it. At this late stage in its development, the contradictions of capitalism are bringing the system to the beginning of its end. Marx's analysis got it right.

But you never hear the "M" word spoken in polite capitalist society or in its impolite punditocracy. Stark Verboten!

So where does that leave us?

With Barack Obama and his $787 billion stimulus package.

There are a number of things that Obama can do to jolt the US and the world economies back into some kind of life.

Everybody knows that Bush's wars, now Obama's wars, are unmitigated catastrophes. So why are they still going on? Save the $40 billion or more a month going down the rat hole for something more rational like single-payer universal health insurance.

Take the costs of providing health care to workers off the backs of business and industry.

Take Cindy Sheehan's advice and end the Iraq and Afghan wars now. Not in sixteen months or nineteen months but now! Get all of our troops out of there. Leave no forces behind as back-up support for the Iraqi government and to prevent a return of al-Qaida. Those are just poor excuses to keep a foot in the door of empire.

Four thousand plus American soldier deaths and more than 31 thousand wounded should never have happened. Cindy Sheehan's son, Casey, should be alive today.

Furthermore, Obama should cut the defense (war) budget in half and close down most of those 700 plus military bases around the world. We can no longer afford to be an imperialist power. We could use that money to rebuild the wrecks we now call public schools.

Still dreaming? Well, let's get real.

Ending the wars? Cutting the defense budget?

> Barack Obama's election campaign pocketed $870,165 from defense-contractor sources, 34% more than the $647,313 in contributions McCain's campaign received from the same sector.
>
> --Time Magazine

Single-payer universal health insurance?

> Obama's campaign collected $18.7 million from the health insurance industry sector, compared to the $7.3 million that his opponent, Republican Sen. John McCain, got.
>
> --opensecrets.org

The Wall Street Journal reported last week (3-5-09) that Physicians for a National Health Program, a group of doctors that claim 15,000 members who support a single-payer system, had planned to demonstrate outside the White House over what they said was the exclusion of single-payer advocates from Obama's Forum on Health Reform held that day.

More than a hundred participants including members of Congress, health insurance lobbyists and representatives of other special interest groups related to health issues attended.

The demonstration was called off, when, at the last minute, the Forum admitted two advocates of the single-payer plan, the head of the physicians group and Rep. John Conyers (D-Mich.) who backs a Medicare-for-All bill in Congress, H.R. 676. A spokesman for the physician's group called it a "small but important victory."

"Health-care reform is no longer just a moral imperative—it's a fiscal imperative," Obama said, master of the cliché and the platitude. He was for a single-payer plan before he was against it.

No way would he now allow single-payer through the gate. He has hinted at other plans for Medicare, like squeezing what he can out of it. So geezers beware before you get busted.

> "The man who has no music in himself
> Nor is not moved with the concord of sweet sounds is
> fit for treason, stratagems and spoils:
> The motions of his spirit are dull as night
> And his affections dark as Erebus.
> Let no such man be trusted."
> **Shakespeare**

It seems that we are all merchants of Venice now.

Finger in the Dike

Why doesn't Barack Obama just put his finger in the dike, as the little Dutch boy did in Holland, to save the dike from crashing and flooding the countryside?

President Obama has a stimulus package. He could shove that in the dyke. There's been a lot of talk about stimulus packages lately but I haven't heard the words "single payer" even once. Nor have I heard the words, "Employee Free Choice Act" being bandied about.

These are two options one would think would be at the top of Obama's list to stimulate the economy. There are others, too, like "repeal Taft Hartley".

I thought the mission here was to create jobs. Obama has been talking about creating four million of 'em in the next two years. Lots of luck! Especially if he is trying to do it without lifting the burden on employers of supplying health care to their workers—or of not actively supporting the rebuilding of the union movement in this country by encouraging collective bargaining, enforcing the Wagner Act and passing Employee Free Choice.

You can't talk about jobs without talking about labor unions. Labor unions protect jobs and are important to job holders because that's the way higher wages are won. And higher wages stimulates the economy because that's the way working families get some purchasing power, some money in their hands so they can buy the stuff that they make.

A good capitalist should know how capitalism works. Just as he has to make sure he has the raw materials to make his product, he has to make sure he has the labor power on hand, no matter how efficient and hi-tech his plant may be. He has to make sure his workers get paid enough to reproduce themselves or he'll have no workers. He also needs them because that's where his profit comes from, the surplus value created by workers. That's the way the system works, Brother. Get used to it, because you're going to hear a lot more about that as the depression deepens. What depression? The one we're in now.

Mr. Obama must have had a very embarrassing moment the other day when Tom Daschle fell out from under him as his Secretary of Health and Human Services—the day the lead editorial in the New York Times revealed that Mr. Daschle had failed to pay over $128,000 in taxes because his benefactor had neglected to give him a 1099 form.

The editorial also revealed that Mr. Daschle "cashed in on his political savvy and influence to earn $5 million in recent years", two million of that from a law and lobbying firm, $2 million from a private equity firm, and "hundreds of thousands of dollars for speeches to interest groups, including those representing health insurance plans, medical equipment distributors and pharmacy boards. Although Mr. Daschle was not a registered lobbyist, he offered policy advice to the UnitedHealth Group, a huge insurance conglomerate. He was also a trustee of the Mayo Clinic in Minnesota."

If there was a heavy odor of conflict-of-interest surrounding the would-be Secretary of Health and Human Services, President Barack Obama apparently wasn't able to sniff it out—or perhaps he had a problem of his own in this area since he was the recipient of $2.2 million contribution from the health insurance industry during his election campaign.

Mr. Daschle took the advice of the New York Times and withdrew his name.

The stimulus bill didn't receive a single Republican vote in the House. The Republicans wanted tax cuts, not a knee-jerk Democratic tax-and-spend bill. President Obama tried to convince the Republicans that stimulus meant spend. That was the point. You stimulate by spending. Don't know if that got through or not.

His sober assessment that this financial crisis could turn into a catastrophe didn't faze the Republicans. They're back in the hen-house now picking away. I would bet that when they're finished there won't be a corn kernel or an earmark left in the bill. Maybe Obama just doesn't know how to handle Republicans.

There is not a kid in all of the Netherlands who doesn't know the story of how Hans Brinker stuck his finger in the dike and saved the country. That little boy represents the spirit of the whole country.

Not a leak can show itself anywhere either in its politics, honor, or public safety, that a million fingers are not ready to stop it, at any cost.

Maybe we can all take a lesson from that.

The Ghost of Times Past

A spectre is haunting America—the spectre of Taft-Hartley.

The Taft-Hartley Act of 1947, otherwise known as The Labor-Management Relations Act, became law in the Truman Administration after World War II, restricting the power of labor unions and clobbering the working class.

During the war, labor had won many victories, achieving higher wages, better working conditions, health benefits and pension plans. Even women were working in defense industries. Remember "Rosie the riveter"?

A real "labor movement" was built in the United States, with the strengthening of the AFL and the creation of the CIO. It contributed to the broadening of the middle class. The workers were winning a round in the class struggle.

Labor's standing was uplifted a decade earlier, in the depth of The Great Depression, when a Senator from New York ushered a bill through Congress that became known as the Wagner Act, officially the National Labor Relations Act, and created the National Labor Relations Board (NLRB) to act on labor matters.

The Act protected the rights of workers in the private sector, establishing the legality to organize labor unions, to engage in collective bargaining, and to take part in strikes and other forms of concerted activities in support of their demands. It was the best thing that had happened to labor in a long time, tending to level the playing field and allowing for a more equitable distribution of wealth. Workers gained the purchasing power with which to buy the products they produced. It kept the economy afloat.

The NLRB was given the power to investigate and decide on charges of unfair labor practices and to conduct elections in which workers would have the opportunity to decide whether they wanted to be represented by a union. The government was on the side of the people, for a change.

Then, Taft-Hartley hit—a McCarthy period bill sponsored by Republican right-wingers, Senator Robert Taft and Rep. Fred Hartley. Taft-Hartley was designed to put labor back in its hole. It was enacted by Congress, overriding President Truman's veto. Labor leaders called it the "slave-labor bill". It pulled the teeth and tore the claws out of the Wagner Act.

Corporate power went on a crusade to crush the organized labor movement in this country. Taft-Hartley was the weapon.

According to the Wall Street Journal they succeeded nicely, "In the US, just 7.5% of private-sector workers are union members." (8-22-08 A11) Now, the economy is down in the hole with the work force.

Instead of building on our industrial and manufacturing base, our greedy and grave-digging capitalists have off-shored their plants and out-sourced our jobs to places where labor costs are lowest; where profits are the only thing that matters. A race to the bottom. We are now importing the products our own workers should be producing.

If you didn't know we've been in a recession for over a year, you haven't been paying attention. The economic collapse facing this country is spreading world-wide.

"We are experiencing an unprecedented economic crisis that has to be dealt with and dealt with rapidly," Obama told reporters on Friday (1-23-09) as he met with lawmakers at the White House. He's trying to get a stimulus package of around $825 billion out of Congress by mid-February. He thinks he can rescue the economy by throwing money at it. The Republicans, of course, want tax cuts.

The first thing Obama should do is get Congress to repeal Taft-Hartley and it wouldn't cost him a dime. If he could help revive the union movement he might get some higher wages in the hands of the working class and create some purchasing power.

The second thing he should do is get the Employee Free Choice Act through Congress. Under the Act, the NLRB would recognize a union's role as an official bargaining agent if a majority of employees authorized representation via a card check (signing a card stipulating their preference), without requiring the cumbersome secret ballot election that has cracked many a union when the employer has purposely tied it up in bureaucratic red tape.

The Employee Free Choice bill got through the House in 2007 and had majority support in the Senate, but was never voted on due to a Republican-led filibuster. President Obama has expressed his support of the measure.

The third thing President Obama should do is make "close shop" and "union shop" mandatory for all infrastructure projects financed by the current stimulus package. Encourage collective bargaining and strengthen the unions. That's been a long-standing tradition on government financed jobs.

The fourth thing the President should do is to make bread and milk free to all families with children living below the poverty line.

It would show that the President cares about people.

What he does with the rest of the 825 Billion dollar stimulus package may help the economy in the short term.

Foreign Entanglements

In this season of farewell addresses and inaugurals, it would be a good time to remember the famous farewell address of George Washington.

Although the advice Washington gave to the fledging nation was "beware of foreign entanglements", he did not used those particular four words in his farewell address. This may be a shock to many who keep quoting him mistakenly.

But there is no doubt about what he meant.

"The nation which indulges toward another an habitual hatred or an habitual fondness is in some degree a slave. It is a slave to its animosity or to its affection, either of which is sufficient to lead it astray from its duty and its interest," said George.

Well, it seems by George Washington's definition, the United States, today, is a slave nation. We have an "habitual hatred" of Iran and an "habitual fondness" for Israel. Couldn't be clearer.

George went on to say, "A passionate attachment of one nation for another produces a variety of evils. Sympathy for the favorite nation, facilitating the illusion of an imaginary common interest in cases where no real common interest exists, and infusing into one the enmities of the other, betrays the former into a participation in the quarrels and wars of the latter without adequate inducement or justification."

Did he mean Israel and the United States? Of course not. Israel didn't exist then. But maybe old George was prescient? Sounds to me like he's describing what's been happening in Gaza the last three weeks.

We certainly have been facilitating Israel's massacre of the people of Gaza by supplying much of the weaponry they have been using and we've been helping them out at the United Nations Security Council.

When Israeli Prime Minister Ehud Olmert can pick up a phone and call George W. Bush, and tell him how to vote on a UN resolution, you know

this country is still a slave state. Olmert did so order Bush how to vote on a cease-fire resolution on Gaza. Bush obeyed and told Condoleezza Rice, his Secretary of State, to abstain from voting on the very resolution that she helped draft. Now that's going beyond Chutzpah!

George Washington, in his farewell address, goes on to talk about politicians, those "deluded citizens who devote themselves to the favored nation." It gives them, he says, "the facility to betray or sacrifice the interests of their own country without odium, sometimes even with popularity... a commendable deference for public opinion, or a laudable zeal for public good the base or foolish compliances of ambition, corruption or infatuation."

Was he talking about the Bush Administration or the neo-cons at the Pentagon?

George continues his farewell address with some more advice for us. "The great rule of conduct for us in regard to foreign nations is, in extending our commercial relations to have with them as little political connection as possible."

How about military connection? George doesn't say much about that. I would say it is an "entanglement".

It is estimated that we have about 751 military bases in about 130 countries, not counting those we have in the two countries, Iraq and Afghanistan, where presumptive wars rage. No one can quite precisely pin down who the enemy is or tell us what "victory" would consist of but that doesn't seem to matter as American soldiers continue to die (over 4000, now) and taxpayer dollars flood out at the rate of about $12 billion a month. When asked what the reason for it is, the government should tell us the truth—profits.

War criminals Dick Cheney and George Bush seem to be about to fly the coop scot-free, but they have their albatrosses around their necks and they never know when the occasion might arise when they will come up and bite them.

Perhaps President-Elect Barack Obama needs a strong perfected warning concerning his aggravated criminal liability for any murders committed either by US military forces or by client states after he assumes office on January 20th.

By some counts, Obama is already a war criminal by vice of his actions in the Senate supporting US aggression against Afghanistan and funding for the occupation of Iraq, to mention two. Unless Obama radically changes course on a dime, there will be a qualitative moment, probably on Tuesday the way things are going now, when the first victim is wantonly slain by US forces a moment after he becomes Commander in Chief. The mantle of war criminal will come fluttering down upon his shoulders as he joins his predecessors waiting for the albatross to bite.

The fact that Obama has surrounded himself with such notorious war-mongers as Joe Biden, Hillary Clinton and Rahm Emanuel, and has kept on Bush's Secretary of War, Robert Gates, shows the overwhelming probability that he will fecklessly disregard any lawful warning, however cogent.

A final piece of advice; perhaps meant for an Obama obeisant to Israel by a prescient George Washington:

"There can be no greater error than to expect or calculate upon real favors from nation to nation. It is an illusion which experience must cure, which a just pride ought to discard."

Card Check

Note to the new prez: a stimulus package won't do you a damn bit of good unless you can create a surge of purchasing power that will raise spending to lofty heights.

Note to the new working class: demography and immigration have now made you the vanguard; Hispanics, Blacks, Asians, Pakistanis, Middle Easterners, Africans, and others who have migrated to the United States to partake in the American dream. The Jews, the Irish, the Italians, the Germans, the Scandinavians, the Slavs and other middle Europeans have moved up the ladder to fresher fields.

The former union leaders are gone, too; the Gene Debs', the David Dubinskys, the Sidney Hillmans, The Walter Reuthers , the John L Lewis', all dim memories.

Today, you are fighting new battles for a fundamental idea—collective bargaining.

The Wagner Act, otherwise known as The **National Labor Relations Act** was passed during the Roosevelt Administration in 1935. It established a Federal law to protect the rights of workers in the private sector to organize unions, to engage in, and encourage, collective bargaining for labor, permit strikes and other forms of concerted activity in support of their demands. The corporate oligarchy, or "economic royalists" as Franklin Roosevelt called them, fought it, tooth and nail, all the way.

The Act worked well for about 50 of its 75 years. The American Federation of Labor (AFL) was one of the first federations of labor unions in the United States, founded by Samuel Gompers in Columbus, Ohio in 1886. The AFL consisted (and still consists) mainly of craft unions.

John L. Lewis, former head of the United Mine Workers, saw industrialism in the US expanding in the first half of the 20ᵗʰ Century. He saw the need for organizing workers in mass production industries. He formed the Congress of Industrial Organizations (CIO), encompassing steel workers, mine, mill and smelter workers, auto workers, electrical and communication workers, and so many others all open to African Americans and other minorities.

Both federations grew rapidly during the Great Depression. By 1955, they merged, forming the new entity known as the American Federation of Labor-Congress of Industrial Organizations (AFL-CIO), as we know it today.

A strong labor movement was welded in the United States that lasted through the 1970s that raised the standard of living for workers. Unions fought for higher wages, better working conditions, health benefits and pension plans. It formed the basis of a broader middle class, the pride of America.

The attack on labor by corporate power was, nevertheless, unrelenting. The "economic royalists", as Roosevelt called the corporate oligarchy at the time, fought the trade union movement from the very beginning. The profit system necessitated squeezing every bit of labor's surplus value out of the worker.

Trade unions were forced to fight for survival with bargaining, boycotts and blood. Most of the time, union violence was provoked by industry, exemplified in 1937 when Chicago police killed ten striking steel workers in a bloody, historic battle—the Memorial Day massacre.

Eventually, of course, the employers succeeded.

You could say that the current problem began with the Reagan "revolution". He struck the first blow by breaking the air-controllers' (PATCO) strike. It proceeded from there. Corporate power went on a crusade to crush the organized labor movement in this country.

Under capitalism, the assault on labor has always been overwhelming, continuous, inhuman and destructive from the beginning of the industrial revolution to this very day. No wonder unions are dysfunctional and chaotic. So are most of their leaders. If they're not coerced, co-opted or corrupted, they're framed, jailed or neutralized in some way. At this stage in our history, corporate America has done a pretty smashing job.

The battle today roils around the attempt in Congress to pass the Employee Free Choice Act. It could give labor organization a fresh boost.

The Act, if passed, would establish a level playing field for workers and union organizers in their struggle against employers and contractors who exploit and intimidate their employees.

Under an Employee Free Choice Act, the National Labor Relations Board (NLRB) would recognize the union's role as the official bargaining agent if a majority of employees authorized representation via a card check (signing a card stipulating their preference), without requiring a secret ballot election.

The bill was passed by the House in 2007 and had majority support in the Senate, but was never voted on due to a Republican-led filibuster.

In the new Obama Administration, passing the EFCA will become a number one priority for organized labor. Barack Obama has expressed his support of the measure.

It would get his stimulus package off to a flying start to see a little more of workers' surplus value lifting purchasing power rather than flowing up into the pockets of the economic royalists.

What Goes Around

What happens when one mighty militarized nation smashes a small, defenseless country?

The United States of America has smashed Iraq. The militarized state of Israel is smashing the Gaza Strip.

We have only to wait for the effect to come around.

In Hinduism, the word Karma defines the universal principle of action and reaction that governs all life—the relationship between one event, called cause, and another, called effect, which is the direct consequence, or result, of the first.

Justin Raimondo, in Antiwar.com (1-5-09), says that this latest aerial assault of shock and awe by the Israelis on the Gaza Strip and the subsequent invasion with tanks and artillery benefits al-Qaeda affiliates and the Israelis; and "the losers are the Palestinians and the American people, with the former enduring the slaughter and the later paying for it. We will pay for it not only in billions of our tax dollars, but in terms of the hate-America factor, which will skyrocket on the Arab 'street' and inspire many to take up arms against us."

We have already seen this in "9/11"—the destruction of the World Trade towers. The glib explanation for it was, "They hate us because we're rich, successful, democratic..." A more reasonable explanation for it would be that our lop-sided foreign policy relating to Israel and the Arab world had a lot to do with building up that hate.

Back in 1933, we had an economic collapse after a stock market crash that led to "the Great Depression". In the 1932 presidential election, Herbert Hoover, Republican incumbent, lost to Franklin D. Roosevelt, Democrat, who was inaugurated in March of 1933. In that interim period between the November election and the inauguration date (later changed to January 20th), the country sank deeper into depression— very much like it is starting to do now, while waiting for the incoming Obama Administration to officially start governing the country.

Roosevelt took immediate action. He put through the Securities Act of 1933, the Glass-Steagall Act of 1933 and the Securities Exchange Act of 1934 to stem the downward spiral.

Glass-Steagall had the greater wallop. It got to the root of the problem. Up to that time, bankers and brokers were sometimes indistinguishable. Congress examined the mixing of the "commercial" and "investment" banking industries that occurred in the 1920s. There were conflicts of interest and fraud in many banking activities. The Glass-Steagall Act set up a stringent barrier to the mixing of these activities as well as establishing the Federal Deposit Insurance Corporation (FDIC) to protect bank deposits.

Glass-Steagall served the country very well for many years. It kept the manipulators and speculators at bay. Like church and state, commercial banking and investment banking must be kept separate.

But, in the 1980s, it fell apart. The "banksters" got the upper hand. The Depository Institutions Deregulation and Monetary Control Act was passed. It started nipping away at Glass-Steagall. A major blow came in

November of 1999. Senator Phil Gramm of Texas, the notorious tax-cutter, led the charge. Provisions that prohibit a bank holding company from owning other financial companies were repealed by the Gramm-Leach-Bliley Act. The bill was signed into law by then-President Bill Clinton. The deregulators had a field day.

Our economy is now in free fall again, with no Glass-Steagall law to rescue it. In effect, we've come around to where we were at the end of the Hoover era in the early 1930s.

There must be a lesson here.

When the first settlers came to America, they found Native American tribes living in a state of primitive communism.

Lewis Henry Morgan, American anthropologist, explored this era in the development of human culture in his classic work, "Ancient Society", published in 1877. He describes the "communism in living" evident in the village architecture of Native Americans.

Friedrich Engels, collaborator of Karl Marx, in his work, "The Origin of the Family, Private Property and the State", published in 1884, was heavily influenced by Morgan's evolutionary history. Engels postulated that primitive communism applied to early human societies because hunter-gatherer cultures did not create surpluses.

In a primitive communist society, all able bodied persons would have engaged in obtaining food, and everyone would share in what was produced by hunting and gathering. There would be almost no private property other than articles of clothing and similar personal items, because primitive society produced no surplus; what was produced was quickly consumed. The few things that existed for any length of time (tools, housing) were held communally. There would have been no state.

Primitive societies may have contained all of the features presently associated with the goals of "communism" as conceived today, exemplified by the Marxist slogan, "from each according to his ability, to each according to his needs". In the Marxist view, such an arrangement will be made possible by the abundance of goods and services that a developed communist society will produce; the idea is that there will be enough to satisfy everyone's needs

With the world now threatened by economic collapse, we may soon find ourselves in a situation where there are no surpluses.

What does this foretell?

Will we be in a state of communism, perhaps less primitive, more sophisticated?

Will we rebuild, but on a higher level?

What went around could come around….

Single Payer Spearhead

Grab the bull by the horns! Not the Merrill Lynch bull, that's already been slaughtered—but the horns of the raging bull known as the Health Insurance Industry. That's what Barack Obama must do in his first hundred days in the Oval Office.

With the economy in free-fall, instituting a single-payer health plan would go a long way in slowing that fall and would win back the support of his base, the liberal and progressive wing of the Democratic Party that won him the election.

Single Payer should be the spearhead of his promised humongous stimulus package. And it would be easy. The infrastructure is there. All he has to do is tell Congress to extend Medicare to all citizens and he would sign the bill.

It would be a bold move. In a single stroke, he would create a great legacy for himself.

His only problem—he would have to bite the hand that fed him. He took millions from the Health Insurance Industry to finance his campaign. They gave him the money to insure that those two verboten words "single payer" would never be mumbled. And they weren't—during the entire campaign.

Now, it is true that back in 2003, when Barack was an Illinois state senator, he spoke to an AFL-CIO group and told them, "I happen to be a proponent of a single payer universal health care plan. I see no reason why the United States of America, the wealthiest country in the history of the world, spending 14 percent of its Gross National Product on health care, cannot provide basic health insurance to everybody." Those were his exact words. It's in the public record.

When Obama threw his hat into the ring in 2008, and the long primary battle with Hillary Clinton for the nomination began, Obama's sentiments seem to have morphed from single payer to "affordable" health care. That means working in alliance with the Health Insurance companies.

None of the candidates have ever used the term "single payer". They had all kept the specifics of their health plans very vague, fudging words like "universal" and "national" and for a very good reason. There was a raging bull out there listening to every word.

Hillary learned her lesson back in 1992 when she and Bill tried to finagle some kind of Rube Goldberg health insurance plan. It angered the bull and the Health Insurance Industry dropped a bomb on them in the form of a TV commercial with Harry and Louise sitting around the kitchen table talking health plans and calling Hillary and Bill's plan "socialized medicine". Heavens to Betsy! Horrors! Socialized Medicine! Hillary and Bill got off that tack real fast and became the Bonnie and Clyde of politics in other areas.

Are we going to go on talking the talk and getting ripped off by Big Insurance and Big Pharma forever? Why can't we have what every other industrialized nation in the world enjoys—some form of national health insurance run by the government, yes...socialized medicine?

The current health insurance system in America violates the very essence of the principle of insurance. Here's how it's supposed to work: you pay a small premium for a large benefit. The more people paying into the pool, the lower will be the premium. The larger the pool, the more efficient the system. So why not the whole country?

In the current US system, there are literally tens of thousands of different, and overlapping health care organizations generating a blizzard of paperwork in an administrative wilderness creating enormous waste. There are thousands, if not millions of people pushing paper around. The overhead is estimated to be over 30%; whereas Medicare operates on an overhead of around 3 or 4%.

A look back at the endless squabble over health care in this country will reveal where this timidity about single payer comes from.

"Socialized Medicine" were the scare words. They were used the way George W. Bush now uses "the war on terror"; to scare the American people into accepting two useless, endless wars in Iraq and Afghanistan.

It was the American Medical Association (AMA), after World War II, that raised the bug-a-boo of "socialized medicine" when they saw something new blowing in the wind—pre-paid medical plans. Organized medicine saw these plans as a threat to their "fee for service" system. (You go to a doctor, you get a service, and you pay a fee) That's the way they wanted to keep it, by God!

It was Henry Kaiser, the auto maker and ship builder, who came up with the idea of a Health Maintenance Organization for his employees—a prepaid medical plan. (You pay a small monthly fee, you get your entire medical and hospital needs free of any other charges)

The City of New York jumped right in with HIP (Health Insurance Plan of Greater New York), a pre-paid health plan for the city employees.

"Socialized Medicine!" screamed the AMA. Physicians and surgeons manned the battle stations. Many saw their seven figure incomes taking flight.

Other HMOs mushroomed around the country. And, then, in 1965, President Lyndon Johnson made "medical care for the aged" part of his "Great Society" package. We know it today as "Medicare". Then, came Medicaid, medical care for the indigent. The flood gates were opened. For the first time, huge amounts of government money started pouring into the health care system.

The insurance companies knew a good thing when they saw it. Organized medicine, the AMA and its state and county medical societies, did not—paralyzed by their fear of government intrusion.

Insurance companies relished the enormous cash flow of government money emanating from Medicare and Medicaid and other government programs like Champus, medical coverage for servicemen and their families.

Insurance companies set up their own private plans, yes, HMOs, to sop up all that loose cash. They turned pre-paid plans into their opposite, not "socialized medicine" for the people, but corporate welfare for the insurance companies. Through the years, they increased premiums and cut services, raking in billions of dollars in profits instead of providing not-for-profit medical services to their subscribers.

The doctors allowed themselves to be co-opted and blind-sided. They allowed the pre-paid plans to get away from them. The fear of "socialized medicine" dimmed their vision. So instead of "socialized medicine" the doctors got privatized sweatshops where some doctors cannot make medical decisions without the approval of an HMO bureaucrat.

Managed care became mismanaged medicine.

Is this the system Barack Obama wants to continue with his "affordable" health care plan, begging the Health Insurance companies for the few crumbs falling from the table while they continue to rake in whopping billions in profits off our backs?

Or will he be a man of principle, take the bull by the horns, come forward with his true beliefs as he expressed them in 2003, and give us the change we can believe in?

Beyond Decadence

The story of Bernie Madoff is the perfect paradigm for morality in the era of monopoly capitalism.

As an investment broker with a "black box", Madoff managed to swindle $50 billion, yes, billion—before being caught. Madoff targeted his own people in the Jewish community and even ripped off charitable organizations that were supporting humanitarian projects in Israel. He used the oldest of the old scams, the Ponzi or pyramid scheme—paying off old investors with exorbitant fictitious interest, money from new investors, while investing nothing.

According to Wikipedia, the Internet encyclopedia, the original schemer was Sarah Howe, who in 1880 opened up a "Ladies Deposit" in Boston promising eight percent interest, although she had no method of making profits. This unique scheme was billed as "for women only." Howe was arrested on October 18, 1880 by New York City Police and sentenced to three years in prison. There have been a myriad of schemers through the decades since then, with stakes getting higher as capitalist greed developed. Wall Street, itself, is a kind of gambling casino where, apparently, pyramid schemers can operate.

What makes it possible?

Greed and negligence.

Greed on the part of the schemer and the public. Negligence on the part of the government and the regulators whose job it is to see to it that our financial markets operate on the up and up—primarily the Security and Exchange Commission (SEC).

Greed is one of the seven deadly sins: lust, gluttony, greed, sloth, wrath, envy and pride. Greed is defined as an excessive desire to acquire or possess more than what one needs or deserves, especially wealth.

As the expression goes, "We all have a little larceny in our hearts".

Does that describe Bernie Madoff, or does that describe his host of victims?

Well, both.

Capitalism brings out the worst in people. People are not monolithic, they are multifaceted.

The Roman Catholic Church recognizes "Seven Virtues" which correspond inversely to each of the seven deadly sins—Chastity for Lust, Temperance for Gluttony, Charity for Greed, Diligence for Sloth, Patience for Wrath, Kindness for Envy and Humility for Pride.

Why can't we be more charitable, less greedy?

We can be if we change the material conditions of our lives—the economic system under which we live—the profit system.

Karl Marx made an astounding discovery that stands with Charles Darwin's theory of evolution and Sigmund Freud's discovery of the Id, the Ego and the Super-ego.

Marx discovered that "The history of all hitherto existing society is the history of class struggles". His monumental analysis of capitalism, "Das Kapital", the first of three volumes published in 1867, described the new mercantile world of capitalism growing out of feudalism, and how the system is based on the exploitation of one class by another (the proletariat or working class by the bourgeoisie or capitalist class) and that "profits" are derived from the surplus value created by labor in the process of production. Capitalism is based on the theft of labor power from the workers by the owners of the means of production.

The main drive of the capitalist is to maximize profits, always trying to squeeze more surplus value out of his workers by cutting wages, increasing hours of work for the same pay, denying benefits and other handy techniques.

The workers' main weapon for fighting back is the strike. But that takes solidarity and unionization, of which there is little around, lately.

The only outstanding recent example is the successful sit-down strike by the workers at the Republic Windows and Doors plant in Chicago. In 1937, there were 733 such sit-in strikes, growing out of the example set by the General Motors workers in Flint, Michigan who closed down 3 GM plants.

The United Auto Workers (UAW) was formed, despite GM's vow to prevent it.

The US developed a strong industrial labor movement with such leaders as John L. Louis, of the United Mine Workers and a leader in the formation of the Congress of Industrial Organizations (CIO) There were many others to follow. A strong union movement, winning higher wages and benefits and a better distribution of wealth, contributed to America's development of a broad middle class.

That was then, this is now.

The onslaught on the labor movement in this country began with the Reagan Administration's attack on the Professional Air Traffic Controllers Organization (PATCO) in 1981.

Twelve thousand air traffic controllers went out on strike for higher wages and better working conditions, setting off a chain of events that would redefine labor relations in America.

On August 3, 1981, President Reagan gave the PATCO strikers 48 hours to return to work. Two days later, when the strikers refused, Reagan carried out his threat. He fired 12,000 controllers and banned them from federal service for three years.

This was a tip-off to employers in the private sector. The government was on their side. The onslaught continued in the intervening years and capital effectively broke the back of the labor movement in this country.

Is there a lesson here, for today—as we head into another great depression?

The lesson may be that we'll have to wait for the crash to come before the working class of America can get organized again.

Meanwhile, greed is the order of the day.

All Roads

Who was it that said "All roads lead to Socialism"?

Was it that German guy with the full head of hair and the bushy beard? The guy, who, with his friend, Freddy Engels, spent a lot of time at the British Museum in London, in mid-Nineteenth Century, studying the results of this new thing called capitalism that mushroomed out of the Industrial Revolution in England?

Yes, it was. And it was the same two guys who wrote "The Communist Manifesto", published in 1848, which said "The history of all hitherto existing society is the history of class struggles". The bushy-bearded German was a man, both praised and reviled, by the name of Karl Marx. He also wrote a book called "Das Kapital" ("Capital" as in Capitalism) that analyzed that system, as it was at that time, and predicted where it would go.

The main thesis of Marx's book is that the capitalist system, in a new mercantile world growing out of feudalism, is based on the exploitation of one class by another and that the main drive of the capitalist is to maximize his "profits."

There are many ways of explaining where profits come from and the capitalist has used them all—his entrepreneurship, his land, his factory, his machines, his technology. All subterfuges.

Every workingman knows that profit is derived from the sweat of his brow. It is the surplus value created by labor in the process of production. And that's the only place it can come from. In effect, capitalism is based on the theft of labor power from the workers by the owners of the means of production. Wow! Why wasn't something done about that?

Another of Marx's predictions—capitalism leads to monopoly through mergers and acquisitions of capital enterprises. And monopoly capitalist states, vying for raw materials and markets, resort to imperialist wars. (we've certainly had a long string of those)

In the end, Marx says, the contradictions of capitalism will bring it down. It will "dig its own grave".

There you have it. I think we're in the grave digging stage right now.

The corporate infrastructure in the United States has become so powerful; the government hardly makes a move without its consent.

The corporate oligarchy that runs this country is made up of various segments of capital within the infrastructure as well as high ranking government officials, members of Congress, parts of academia, and other elements within the society. The mainstream media, mostly owned by five major corporate conglomerates, controls most of what we see, hear, and read.

Corruption within the infrastructure is pervasive. Need we mention Blagojevich and Madoff, for starters? Just about every elected politician is in one corporate pocket or another. The political system is fueled by campaign contributions. Politicians need money to get elected and the special interests that give it to them gets a quid pro quo. Everybody knows that's the way the system works.

Alexander Cockburn of the Internet's Counterpunch (12-14-08) reports "The Washington Post congratulates Obama for steering clear of the slime of Chicago politics, but what actually happened is that Obama moved to richer pastures… campaign contributions from the Pritzkers, the Crown family, the big ethanol interests in the Midwest, the nuclear industry, Wall Street financiers, the biggest of big time money, now gratefully acknowledged in the form of Obama's cabinet appointments. Obama raised more money than any presidential candidate in the history of American politics, and here we are getting excited about Rod Blagojevich?"

Barack Obama, our president-elect, crawled out of the Milton Friedman den at the Chicago school of economics where economists still exhorted laissez-faire and deregulated capitalism going back to Adam Smith. "I'm a market man," Obama chortled when he threw his hat into the ring.

After a year in recession, the country is well on its way to an apple sale. The cookie is beginning to crumble, the economy out of control— unemployment and foreclosures shooting up, purchasing power spiraling down. Pretty soon we'll be looking like the "Great Depression" of the 1930s, only worse. Most of the MSM and their pundits are predicting it, even the media whores.

How do we fix it? Everybody's got a plan we know won't work.

The buzz word is "bail out". They are using our taxpayer money, our national treasury, to bail out failing Wall Street firms to the tune of $700 billion. President-elect Barack Obama joined the hunt. President Bush, the decider, and his Secretary of the Treasury, Hank Paulson, can't decide on how to do it. Bush is talking now of diverting some of that money to bail out the auto industry—GM, Ford and Chrysler, the pillars of our manufacturing resources, on the eve of destruction. To save them from collapse, we must fork over $14 billion, just for starters.

To secure these loans, the failing companies will turn over shares of their stock to the government. We are becoming part owners of these companies! Members of the bourgeoisie! Is that socialism sneaking in the back door?

On January 20th, and the inauguration of President Obama (with right wing bigot and evangelical fundamentalist, Pastor Rick Warren reading the invocation—the first voice of the Obama Administration—Barack is going to find a big dump on his new desk in the Oval Office.

Obama has already let us know that he is preparing an humungous stimulus package to save the country. Everybody knows it won't work.

As the economy spirals downward, as the pundits have predicted, we will see more corporations and industries in need of bailouts and take-overs by government.

That's nationalization, isn't it? Also called "socialism".

That's the easy way. The other way is revolution.

As the man with the beard said, "All roads lead to Socialism".

The Plight of the Wishful Thinkers

The Pentagon is preparing to deploy 20,000 federal troops within the United States, presumably to respond to a terrorist attack, but also preparing for the repression of domestic demonstrations, civil disobedience and riots which may result from the predicted economic collapse.

This flies in the face of the Posse Comitatus Act, in force for 130 years. The Act was passed in 1878 at the end of the Reconstruction period after the Civil War. It was designed to prevent federal troops from rampaging through southern states after Reconstruction and has persisted ever since to guarantee states rights. Posse Comitatus prohibits the federal military from acting in a law enforcement capacity. Domestic problems must be handled by local or state police. The Act specifically makes the use of the military by the federal government, within the borders of the United States, unlawful.

But that doesn't seem to mean much to the Bush Administration. They are opening the door for federal troops to engage in law enforcement. You can expect many more to come through.

Does this portend a police state for America?

Will Barack Obama become an outlaw, like his predecessor, if he allows the violation of Posse Comitatus to stand after he takes office?

Will Barack Obama become a war criminal, like his predecessor, if he allows the war in Iraq and Afghanistan to continue, under his Administration, by his selection of the Bushian secretary of "defense", Robert Gates?

And what about Hawk Hillary as the new Obamaian Secretary of State? Iran, beware!

And the new National Security team led by hard-nose General Jim Jones?

And the new Economic team, Citigroup's Robert Rubin, Treasury Secretary's Tim Geithner and Larry Summers, the very ones who participated in bringing the Wall Street debacle down upon us?

Barack Obama is a very creative man. He has formulated an original concept—and he calls it the "team of rivals" offense. If you want to put through a bunch of liberal programs, surround yourself with a bunch of reactionaries. You are the boss-man so they will carry out your orders. This is a reverse logical I have never seen in politics before.

The Obama crowd has put out a set of talking points hyping this "rival team" concept and I have heard some of his gullible left-leaning liberal supporters mouthing them.

It's ironic that the corporate oligarchy chose Barack Obama to lead America into corporatism.

Corporatism? Sounds ominous...

That's how Benito Mussolini, the pre-World War II dictator of Italy, defined fascism. When the corporate oligarchy surrounds and controls the government, the resulting state of governance is called fascism. Mussolini should know. He coined the word.

Fascism? In the USA? Heaven forbid!

When just about every Congressman and Senator is in some corporate pocket, and our new President-elect has been custom made and whipped into place by ubiquitous propaganda including the subservient mainstream media—and when a little scrappy Middle East state wags the big floppy dog, you know that our historical democracy has taken a powder.

Our President-elect Obama, apostle of change, has gone back to the future, bringing the past with him into our future.

Many Americans, who voted for him, did not get what they thought they were getting.

And whose fault was that? Well, the benighted wishful thinkers, of course, the left-leaning liberals and progressives who failed to see what was before their eyes because of their wishful thinkedness.

When will the scales fall from their eyes? Perhaps never—if they haven't yet.

How did this happen?

Well, Senator Barack Obama (D) of Illinois wanted to become president. The oligarchy was casting around for a candidate. After eight years of George W. Bushwhacking, the Democrats were a shoo-in. Their first choice, early on in the 2008 campaign, was Hillary Rodham Clinton, a sure shot. Then this charming, charismatic young man came along with all the qualifications. He was taken up by the oligarchy and his captivating liberal rhetoric enamored the left. His chances to talk Hillary down, during the primary fight, were good; which was exactly what happened.

McCain? No contest.

The selection of Joe Biden as running mate—and the choice of Rahm Emanuel as Chief of Staff, told the whole story.

Joe Biden, establishment hack from Delaware, the state of easy corporate charters, Senator from MasterCard, compulsive plagiarist, even distinguished himself as a warmonger from the Balkan to the Afghan to the Iraq wars.

Rahm Emanuel, Democrat from Illinois's 5th congressional district, scrappy street fighter, noted for his combative style and his political fundraising abilities, is also a personal friend of Obama.

The mainstream media has jumped on the bandwagon. The New York Times, in its lead editorial (12/2/08) says, "There is no underestimating the challenges facing Mr. Obama, and he will need a strong team to help him. The choices announced on Monday are a strong start."

Can you believe that?

"Change we can believe in," was Obama's mantra during the campaign. Mr. Obama's idea of change is no change at all.

It should have been obvious to everyone—but, apparently, not to the wishful thinkers. Their "rival team" talking points don't seem to be doing the job.

What's a left-leaning liberal to do?

The Cookie Crumbles

Does anyone really know what's happening to us right now?

Is it a fiscal crisis or a credit crunch? A recession or a depression? A complete blow-out, maybe a world economic collapse?

Government officials, economists in the know, and media pundits are pouring out a torrent of words trying to explain what's up.

Will the $700 billion bailout of Wall Street do the trick?

There are a slew of opinions on what to do about a sinking auto industry. They now tell us that Citigroup, a giant Wall Street gang of companies, is loaded with toxic assets and needs a bailout.

Despite all the talk, you rarely hear the word "capitalism" and no one is saying, "It's the system, stupid!"

John Molyneux, a British Marxist and lecturer at Portsmouth University, says, "Capitalism is a mass of interlocking contradictions."

Maybe we're caught in one of those?

"There is the contradiction between the capitalist class and the working class, rooted in the exploitation that takes place in every capitalist workplace," says Molyneux.

How does that affect us?

You could say that the current problem began with the Reagan "revolution". He struck the first blow by breaking the air-controllers' strike. It proceeded from there. The corporate oligarchy went on a crusade to crush the organized labor movement in this country.

Under capitalism, the assault on labor has always been overwhelming, continuous, inhuman and destructive from the beginning of the industrial revolution to this very day. No wonder unions are dysfunctional and chaotic. So are most of their leaders. If they're not coerced, co-opted or corrupted, they're framed, jailed or neutralized in some way. At this stage in our history, corporate America has done a pretty smashing job.

Only when capitalism is in the throes of crisis, deep depression and near collapse can labor leaders like Eugene V. Debs or John L. Lewis emerge.

Debs organized the American Railway Union, an industrial union for all railroad workers in 1893, became a confirmed Socialist while serving time in prison for refusing to comply with a federal court injunction, ran for president of the United States four times on the Socialist Party ticket, the last time from prison in 1920 and received nearly a million votes.

John L. Lewis led the United Mine Workers in organizing most of the coal

industry; was one of the organizers of the Congress of Industrial Organizations (CIO) in 1936 and joined the Reuther brothers, Walter and Victor, in organizing the United Auto Workers' sit-in strikes against General Motors at their Flint, Michigan plants.

For 44 bitterly cold winter days the auto workers in Flint held out, eventually inspiring more than two-thirds of General Motors 145 thousand other production workers to strike as well, at dozens of other plants. The strikers in Flint seized, shut down and occupied one, then two, and then three of the key GM plants. Suddenly, workers everywhere were sitting-down. There were 477 sit-down strikes by the end of 1937, involving more than half a million workers.

Mighty GM had vowed publicly that it would never allow the UAW to represent its employees. But the General Motors Corporation ended up granting that crucial right—and more—to the union. It was a stunning victory for the United Auto Workers. It led the way—and swiftly—to the unionization of workers throughout heavy industry and, ultimately, to unionization in all fields. It certainly was the high water mark of labor power in America.

"The fact is capitalism cannot do without the working class; it needs it to produce its profits. And the more capitalism grows and expands, the more it is compelled to increase the size and potential power of its mortal enemy," says Molyneux.

One of the glaring contradictions of capitalism is the need to maximize profits by cutting labor costs. Since profits are derived from the surplus value created by workers in the process of production, lowering wages means less purchasing power for workers to buy the goods that they produce.

We're feeling the pain of that, right now. There'll be no bonanza in the shopping spree this Christmas season. In fact, some of the big-box stores, like Circuit City, are folding their tents and disappearing into the night.

Another contradiction—skyrocketing technology enormously increases the productivity of labor—more production with fewer workers. Only through collective bargaining by strong unions can workers get a fairer share of the value produced.

Barack Obama has a golden opportunity if his left-liberal, progressive supporters whose votes were instrumental in his election to the presidency, have the clout to push him in the left direction.

Everybody knows that the "single payer" health plan is the only plan that can bring universal health care to America as it has for just about every other industrialized nation. But that means taking on the health insurance industry. The Clintons got their fingers burnt trying to do it in the '90s. Will Obama have the guts to do it now?

Will he have the "cohones" to do some other things, like end wars, and bring a little bit of socialism to America, following the Roosevelt New Deal model, thereby saving capitalism for the capitalists?

Who was it that said, "All roads lead to socialism"?

"The bourgeoisie can win battle after battle but it cannot win, or end, the class war," says Molyneux. "The class struggle can end only with the overthrow of the bourgeoisie and the abolition of capitalism."

That's the way the cookie crumbles.

Down the Slippery Slope

Caught again in the American corporate two-party trap, Americans had the glorious choice of voting for the lesser of two evils one more time.

The 2008 Presidential election, the main attraction under the big top, was one of many circuses in our recent history. The two corporate candidates danced upon the stage while the puppet masters pulled their strings for the entertainment of the crowd.

The oligarchy that runs this country is always in a win-win situation. They dole out their power and their money as they judge the effectiveness of the contenders within the prison of the two-party one-party system.

"Hello, my fellow prisoners…" said John McCain, starting one of his campaign speeches with an embarrassing Freudian slip. On several occasions, McCain called Obama "a socialist". He used it as a slur—a dirty word. Socialist. As in Communist. And now Liberal has joined the axis of evil.

Although a Republican is usually their candidate of choice, in this election, the oligarchy felt that Democrat Barack Obama would better serve their agenda.

The election campaign demonstrated one thing, for sure, Barack Obama is a master of the cliché and the platitude. He can weave them in a seamless fine sounding rhetoric. But there is no substance. No fire in the belly.

"Campaign contributions" are the operative words. Corporate sponsors poured on the money in unstinting amounts. Obama had four times the amount McCain had to buy the election. Even in the last days of the campaign, Obama picked up another $150 million.

Another windfall for Obama was the youth vote. They came out in droves to vote for a charismatic black man. It had a democratic flavor. They did not come out as a "youth movement" or organize around popular political issues, with slogans like: "Bring the troops home, NOW!" No, none of that. They came out as individuals, prodded by the Obamaniacs. "I cast my vote. I did my duty. Now let George do it. Obama, of course, is George.

That wasn't the spirit of the youth of the 60s and the 70s. No way! There were organizations on every college campus. There were marches on Washington to end the Vietnam War. There was fire in the belly. Grass roots organization ended the war and forced the resignation of Nixon. But that was then and this is now.

What ever happened to the left? We're a bird flying on a single wing! The defining word. Apathy.

After eight years of Clinton and eight years of Bush (installed by the oligarchy) we're on the edge of the abyss, and President-Elect Barack Obama, carried to victory by many liberal and progressive votes, is looking into the face of the coming world economic collapse. It could well be the end of capitalism as we know it.

There were two similar occasions, in recent memory, but on a lesser scale—Germany in the 1920s and the United States in the 1930s.

Defeat in World War I and the harsh reparations imposed in the Treaty of Versailles destroyed the German economy.

German corporate enterprises—I.G. Farben, Thyssens, Krupps—took over the German government which led to fascism and the eventual rise of Hitler who served the interests of his "enablers", extremely useful for capitalists' purposes.

The Great Depression in the United States in the 1930s, on the other hand, brought Franklin Delano Roosevelt to the fore in the election of 1932, defeating Herbert Hoover, darling of the "economic royalists".

Roosevelt took a different tack. The country was in a state of deflation. It needed immediate resuscitation. And FDR did it. His slogan, "Soak the Rich!"

He raised taxes on the upper brackets to over 90%. He kept the economic royalists in check and brought "socialism" to America. It was the government and not the private sector that did the job. The New Deal. The NRA. The Works Progress Administration. The CCC and the TVA. He put people to work rebuilding the infrastructure of this country. He saved capitalism for the capitalists in the United States.

Barack Obama could follow one of these two models in the current crisis —Germany in the 1920s—the United States in the 1930s.

Which will Obama follow—if either? Barack voted for the $700 billion bailout of Wall Street. Was that Socialism for the rich—coming to America through the back door?

Despite his campaign rhetoric for change, Obama has made it quite clear where he stands on many issues and most of them are not too far from the status-quo. Running down the laundry list, he's for taking troops out of Iraq slowly and keeping some there indefinitely to protect (US?) interests.

On Iran, all options, apparently, are still on the table. Obama is still talking tough on Iran's nuclear program despite the fact the NIE (National Intellegence Estimate) of the US Intelligence Agencies states that Iran had discontinued its nuclear program in 2003. Is Obama taking this stance for Israel's sake? Is he still wagging the dog?

Domestically, he has changed his stance on eavesdropping on American citizens. Are there terrorists among us? He now supports FISA (warrantless surveillance) and giving immunity to the telecommunications companies that participate.

The list goes on.

In addition, an early tip-off of Obama's fundamentals was his selection of running mate, Senator Joe Biden. (Or perhaps the oligarchy made this choice for him.)

Biden is the man from Delaware, the state with loose regulations that has become the corporate charter capital of the world. Biden, the Senator from MasterCard, now faces a credit card crunch similar to the recent sub-prime mortgage crisis. Biden, a hawk and warmonger of long standing, called for attacking Iraq in 2002, a year before Bush got around to it. The oligarchy thought Biden would give Obama some foreign policy credentials.

Obama, after becoming President-Elect of the United States of America, picked as his Chief of Staff, Rep. Rahm Emanuel, Democratic Congressman from Illinois's 5th Congressional District.

Emanuel, a scrappy Chicago street fighter and good friend of Obama, brings with him his checkered background. Emanuel supported the October 2002 congressional resolution authorizing the war in Iraq, differentiating himself from all nine other Democratic members of the Illinois delegation.

According to Wikipedia, the Internet encyclopedia, "Emanuel has been described as a 'strong Israel partisan…a strong supporter of AIPAC, the Israeli Lobby in Washington, he personally introduced Obama to the organization's directors during the 2008 presidential campaign." Rahm's father, Benjamin M. Emanuel, was a pioneer Zionist, a member of the Irgun, a terrorist militia, active during the period of the British Mandate of Palestine between 1931 and 1948.

This is only the beginning. There are many more appointments to come.

Fasten your seat-belts. It's going to be a rough ride.

The Holocaust Next Door

Is there anything more unthinkable than for a people who had suffered the unthinkable, to do unto others what hath been done unto them?

How can you explain the actions of the IDF (the Israeli Defense Forces) blowing up the power plant of Gaza that supplies electricity and power for pumping water to 42% of Gaza's 1.4 million residents? The reason given for that atrocity, according to Israeli officials: it was necessary to make it harder to move around Corporal Gilad Shalit, the 19-year-old Israeli soldier kidnapped by a militant group within Hamas. The Israelis have been on an unprecedented manhunt to retrieve the corporal.

Even Rafik Maliha, the Palestinian manager of the blown up plant, as quoted by the NY Times, said, "Nobody understands the logic. They want to keep people in the dark so kidnappers don't move? What's the relationship?"

Mahmoud Abbas, the Palestinian president, the man the Israelis would prefer to deal with, but whose power had been downsized when Hamas won a parliamentary majority in the recent election, said he considered "the aggression that targeted the civilian infrastructure as collective punishment and a crime against humanity."

Israel has openly announced that "the IDF will continue to employ all means at its disposal to combat terrorists and their infrastructure, in order to defend the citizens of Israel and will continue to make every effort to return Corporal Shalit home quickly and safely."

"We must understand that this campaign against terror is an ongoing struggle. We must continue to do whatever is needed in order to deal with the terror organizations, and complete our mission," said the Chief of General Staff, Lieutenant General Dan Halutz.

Did the General mean that to complete his mission the Palestinian population of the Gaza strip and all of the occupied West Bank, for that matter, must be starved out or driven out of the territory?

Where is the outrage? There's some outcry over the genocide in Darfur. There was some over ethnic cleansing in Kosovo and Bosnia. But what about the Palestinians?

Palestinians have been fighting this relentless drive to get rid of them for more that half a century. We've heard about the endless and deceitful "peace process" *ad nauseum*, and the debates around the two state, and one state and no state solution. All of it meaningless because none of the bottomless pit negotiations have been carried on in good faith. Now we're coming to the end of line.

Right now, it seems like the Israelis have entered a new phase in their longstanding campaign for a "Greater Israel". They're out to break the back of the Hamas government, which the Israelis don't consider a government at all but rather a terrorist regime. Israeli forces have seized more than two-dozen Hamas lawmakers and members of Parliament and are holding them, ostensibly, as bargaining chips for the release of Cpl. Gilad Shalit, but actually for deeper reasons, as revealed by Lieutenant General Dan Halutz's statement.

The term "terrorist" was a favorite appellation of the former tough-minded Prime Minister Ariel Sharon, and the present PM, Ehud Olmert, is carrying on the tradition. Who was it that coined the phrase, "One man's terrorist is another man's freedom fighter"?

Looking back over the 20th century, no fewer than three Israeli prime ministers have been accused of terrorism: Menachem Begin, whose Irgun blew up the King David Hotel and carried out the massacre of Palestinian villagers in Deir Yassin in April of 1948. Yitzhak Shamir, head of the Stern Gang that murdered Edward Lord Moyne in Cairo in 1944 and assassinated U.N. mediator Count Bernadotte in Jerusalem in 1948. Ariel Sharon, as head of Force 101, is accused of massacring scores of Palestinian villagers at Qibya in 1953 in a reprisal raid for the murder of an Israel woman and her children—to say nothing of Sharon's role in the Sabra and Shatila refugee camp massacres by Lebanon Phalangists in 1982. Israel's own Kahan Commission found Ariel Sharon, among other Israelis, as bearing "personal responsibility" for those events.

So who's a terrorist? And who's a freedom fighter?

The British imperialists (and other lesser empire builders) did their part in muddying that distinction. With their empires, they messed up every continent around the world, redrawing national boundaries to suit their interests. The damage resulting from those days of glory are still with us today.

The Palestinians' modern day troubles began while living under British rule, a League of Nations mandate after World War I. On November 2, 1917, before the war even ended, along came the Balfour Declaration and the Palestinians went from the frying pan into the fire. The British yielded to the growing Zionist pressure to carve out a piece of territory where Jews could settle and finally call home after 5000 years of wandering in the Diaspora.

Writer Theodor Hertzl, a Hungarian Jew, founded the Zionist movement in 1896 when he published Der Judenstaat (The Jewish State), calling for the establishment of a national Jewish state.

Chaim Weizmann, a Russian Zionist and a chemist, living in England, met Lord Balfour in 1906. Weizmann began a campaign to convince Balfour that Palestine should be the Jewish National Homeland, but Balfour tried to convince Weizmann that the Zionist movement should accept Uganda, rather than Palestine. Weizmann turned that one down. Good for him.

But it was Weizmann, the chemist, who came through and made all the difference. During World War I, Weizmann formulated the solvent, acetone, using a fermentation process. This was a chemical needed for the war effort and Weizmann won the plaudits of the British military. He struck a chord with the British government, and immediately started working on a proposal for a Jewish Homeland in Palestine. Several factions in the British government wholeheartedly supported the proposal because they saw Palestine as an effective outpost for guarding the Suez Canal.

So, in a way, you can say that the State of Israel, today, owes its existence to acetone. Chaim Weizmann broke the back of the homeland dilemma.

Will it be the 19-year old soldier, Cpl. Gilad Shalit, who will break the camel's back—the world's patience with the genocidal behavior of the State of Israel?

Grave Diggers

I didn't believe I'd ever see it.

Grave diggers at work.

It's an honest profession, I know. Bodies need to be buried. Right now they're working at a frantic pace. You can barely hear the moaning for the swishing of the shovels.

There are bodies lying all around. Lehman Brothers (both of them), Merrill Lynch, Wachovia, Wells Fargo, Citigroup, Goldman Sachs, and other familiar names we've seen on television. Some of the dying are trying to survive by clinging to each other. They can come up with all kinds of Byzantine arrangements. But most of them are too far gone. They need to be gotten out of the way before the stench of the toxic assets becomes overwhelming.

Spurred on by their foreman, Hank Paulson, who is only the Secretary of the Treasury, the diggers are working at breakneck speed. You've got Bob Rubin, one time arbitrage expert for Goldman Sachs, an old crony of Hank and a pal of Bill Clinton in whose administration he learned to swing a shovel. You've got Joe Cassano, formerly Chief Executive Officer of American International Group's Derivatives Unit. Cassano's business was underwriting a huge proportion of the global credit bubble – including the vast American subprime mortgage market. And as house prices in the US fell, the AIG books began to unravel. You've got Richard Fuld, Jr. Chairman and Chief Executive Officer of Lehman Brothers Holdings, Inc., under Chapter 11 Bankruptcy protection, one brokerage firm the government didn't think worth bailing out. You've got John J. Mack, Morgan Stanley's chief. The New York Times says Jack Mack, just "cannot catch his breath". His bank was hit hard by the wallop of the market, its share price plummeting 26% to $12.45. Jack angered many hedge funds by getting regulators to restrict short sellers. It didn't last long. Within twenty-four hours, regulators lifted the temporary ban. But Jack wasn't out of the woods. His cohorts were at him again when Morgan Stanley tried a Hail Mary by fomenting a deal to raise $9 billion from Mitsubishi UFJ in Japan but with the way the market is there, it doesn't look too promising. But Jack is pretty good at wielding a shovel.

Back in the middle of the 19th Century, a young man in Germany with a full head of hair and a bushy beard predicted all this would happen.. He made the most extensive analysis of the workings of the capitalist system to that time. He wrote a book called "Das Kapital"; its first volume was published in 1867.

When the authorities didn't like what they read, they kicked Karl Heinrich Marx out of Germany. He spent most of the rest of his life in Paris, Brussels and London meeting with other budding socialists and making trouble. He participated in the organization known as the International Workingmen's Association, otherwise known as the "First International". He also finished writing the other three volumes of his book with his collaborator, Friedrick Engels.

They spent a lot of time at the British Museum in London.

Marx predicted that the clash, under capitalism, would come between the bourgeoisie and the working class. You don't hear those words today—bourgeoisie—working class. No Siree. You hear entrepreneur—working families—working together as one big family, we are told. That's because the bourgeoisie (establishment) doesn't want you to understand the nature of the class struggle or to question where "profit" comes from.

That's the question. What is the source of profit?

It was a monumental discovery of Marx. It was a discovery that ranked with Sir Isaac Newton's discovery of universal gravitation and the three laws of motion, Charles Darwin's theory of evolution and Sigmund Freud's ego, super-ego and the id.

Profit, Marx proved, is the gain capitalists receive by paying workers less than the full value of their labor. Here's how it works: In a free labor system, under capitalism, labor is a commodity like any other. You pay your worker a wage that represents only a part payment for the value he produces. You have only to extract the surplus value that the worker contributes to the making of the product. You call it profit and say it is derived from entrepreneurial skill, reward for taking risks, from the machinery, the land, or other such gibberish. Once you extract the surplus value the worker creates, let him be free to go his own way and the devil take the hindmost. There is always a plentiful supply of labor to be had.

What! Our revered capitalist system is based on out-and-out thievery! The capitalist steals the surplus value of the labor the worker puts into the commodity being produced! What a discovery!

Marx made another earthshaking discovery. "The history of all hitherto existing society is the history of class struggles". Marx argued that capitalism, like previous socioeconomic systems, will produce internal tensions which will lead to its destruction. "What the bourgeoisie, therefore, produces, above all, are its own grave-diggers. Its fall and the victory of the proletariat are equally inevitable."

Is that what we're seeing now in the USA?

We're a long way from socialism even though we're nationalizing part of our financial structure. Perhaps Socialism is sneaking in through the back door. It might not be such a bad idea!

Under capitalism, the assault on labor has been overwhelming, continuous, inhuman and destructive from the beginning of the industrial revolution to this very day. No wonder unions are dysfunctional and chaotic. So are most of their leaders. If they're not coerced, co-opted or corrupted, they're framed, jailed or neutralized in some way. Only when capitalism is in the throes of crisis, deep depression and near collapse can labor leaders like Eugene V. Debs or John L. Lewis emerge.

Marx believed that capitalism, like previous economic systems will lead to its own destruction. Capitalism cuts from under its own feet the very foundation on which it produces and appropriates products. What it creates, in the process, is its own grave-diggers.

Just as capitalism replaced feudalism, capitalism, itself, will be replaced by another form, be it communism or some form of socialism allowing for a public and private sector in the economy.

There are few parts of the world that were not significantly touched by Marxist ideas in the course of the twentieth century.

Empire in Extremis

⌒∿⌒

"...they stab it with their steely knives,
But they just can't kill the beast..."
-- the Eagles
Hotel California

How many Americans know the actual number of US military bases their tax dollars support around the world?

What would be your guess?

Would you believe 737, spread over 130 countries, according to the Defense Department's annual "Base Structure Report"—and that's not counting another 6000 bases in the United States and its territories?

Chalmers Johnson, in his latest book, "Nemesis: The Last Days of the American Republic" cites the "worldwide total of U.S. military personnel in 2005, including those based domestically, to be 1,840,062 supported by an additional 473,306 Defense Department civil service employees and 203,328 local hires."

Overseas bases, according to the Pentagon, contained 32,327 barracks, hangars, hospitals, and other buildings, which it owns, and 16,527 more that it leases; and more than 29,819,492 acres of land worldwide, making the Pentagon one of the world's largest landlords.

The Roman Empire at its height in the year 117 AD had only 37 bases to police its realm from All Gaul (which was divided into three parts) to Egypt.

Ike Eisenhower's parting shot, when he left the presidency of the United States in 1961, was his warning about the military-industrial complex.

It was too little, too late. We had been a nation born in genocide, destroying the Native American tribes and taking possession of their land. We developed a major part of our economy through slavery, a plantation system and a three way slave trade broken only by the industrial revolution and the development of capitalism. The Civil War brought us into the modern imperialist era. The Monroe Doctrine. Manifest Destiny.

We allowed ourselves to become a militarized nation, a militarized economy. We needed to set an example for the world. Any defiance of our hegemony meant war. There was the Mexican War. The Spanish-American War. We took Cuba and the Philippines. It went on from there.

So now we have a war-like beast that cannot be restrained. Slick propaganda got us into World War I and Pearl Harbor into World War II (conveniently arranged, some say). The Korean War and the Vietnam War were set-ups. Dominoes just don't fall that way. But we've managed to leave military bases in the lands of most of the vanquished, in South Korea and in Germany, to name a few, still there after fifty and sixty years.

US elder statesman of finance, Alan Greenspan, former head of the Federal Reserve, has finally admitted, in his recently published memoir, that the Iraq War was primarily about oil (something the Bush administration has vehemently denied).

So our simple democracy has spawned a global empire.

What does this portend?

Must we start another war to keep the economy going? Bush would like to get someone to bomb Iran before he leaves office. Maybe he can get Israel to do it? They've been champing at the bit, just waiting for the nod from Bush. But even the Israelis must be struck by what a world-wide catastrophe the bombing of Iran would cause.

So what is a nation to do?

This nation must militate! Like Mussolini did in Italy. A little Fascism might be a helpful thing. Make the planes fly on time. It could also keep activists in their place. Inactive. They didn't build Guantanamo for nothing. America's first concentration camp? No, it's second. There were the Japanese relocation centers during World War II.

And extraordinary rendition might also be a useful tool to keep the lid on. A little kidnapping. A little torture by proxy, off-shore.

Does it fit the Project for the Old American Century criterion for fascism, comparing the regimes of Hitler, Mussolini, Franco, Suharto, and Pinochet and the 14 characteristics common to those fascist regimes? Well, maybe not all—but enough.

You must glorify war in order to get the public to accept the fact that they're going to send their sons and daughters to die. And don't forget to wear your lapel flag pin.

There was a little juice in the anti-war movement before the onslaught on Iraq in 2003. But then it went blah. What happened?

In the mid-term election of 2006, the Democrats took both houses of Congress. Polls showed that a majority of Americans, some as high as 73%, wanted an end to the Iraq war and they counted on the Democrats to get it for them.

What they got was a continuation of the war with enough Democrats joining the Bush War Party to vote for funding. Among them were

Hillary Clinton and Barack Obama who, in the midst of their primary squabble over who was the most anti-war, both voted to fund the war. That's the kind of steely knives they used!

We now have two presidential candidates representing different wings of the ruling oligarchy. You're trapped in our two party-one party system.

> "...you can check-out any time you like,
> But you can never leave!"

Life, Liberty and
the Pursuit of Change

The American people want change!

They're entitled to it. It's written into their Constitution.

The two presumptive candidates for president, in the upcoming 2008 election, both believe in change.

John McCain, the Republican, believes in climate change. He's said so many times. Barack Obama, the Democrat, believes in change we can believe in.

Polls show that the #1 issue weighing on the minds of Americans today is the collapsing economy. How do you stop the free fall we're experiencing now? If it lands it could make a hole in the ground that will make 1932 look like an apple sale on the street?

George W. Bush must have been chuckling to himself when he signed Congress' economic stimulus package, sending out $300 to $1200 rebate checks. Maybe he thinks that's the way to keep the flow of wealth upwards.

Americans need purchasing power worth a damn! They need jobs like those they had when there was a strong labor movement in this country and good, high paying wages in manufacturing won through blood and guts and strikes.

The Reagan revolution ended all that.

Reagan mercilessly broke the air traffic controllers when they went out on strike. That kicked off the onslaught.

The corporate oligarchy took their shot. They undercut the unions by off-shoring factories and out-sourcing jobs.

As Ross Perot described it when he was running for president in 1992, you could hear the "sucking sound" as jobs and plants went flying off to countries that paid the lowest wages. It was a race to the bottom and the beginning of what we now call "globalization." They hollowed out the country for profits. They exported their plants and brought back their products as imports. That gave a strong manufacturing base to our foreign competitors and piddling wages at service jobs to American workers. "Yeah, I work at McDonalds, but I can buy cheap at Walmart's".

According to the Bureau of Labor Statistics, union membership, nationwide, was down to 12 percent in 2007. There was a time when things were different. In the mid 1950's more than 35 percent of all employees on private payrolls were union members.

We had some great labor leaders in our time. There was the great Eugene Debs who organized the American Railway Union in 1893. He wanted to see change in the country, too. He ran for President of the United States four times on the Socialist Party ticket, the last time from prison in 1920 and received nearly one million votes.

And then there was the great John L. Lewis, head of the mine workers, who organized the Congress of Industrial Organizations (CIO) and created great change. He brought industrial unionism to this country for the first time.

In 1936, Lewis joined the Reuther brothers, Walter and Victor, in organizing

the United Auto Workers' sit-in strikes against General Motors at their Flint, Michigan plants.

For 44 bitterly cold winter days the auto workers in Flint held out, eventually inspiring more than two-thirds of General Motors 145 thousand other production workers to strike.

Change came to Flint and the auto industry with a bang. The strikers seized, shut down and occupied one, then two, and then three of the key GM plants. Suddenly, workers everywhere were sitting-down. There were 477 sit-down strikes by the end of 1937, involving more than half a million workers. What hath change wrought!

Mighty GM had vowed publicly that it would never allow the UAW to represent its employees. But the General Motors Corporation ended up granting that crucial right—and more—to the union. It was a stunning victory for the United Auto Workers.

The two major union organizations united. The AFL-CIO was formed. Solidarity! It led the way—and swiftly—to the unionization of workers throughout heavy industry and, ultimately, to unionization in all fields. It brought higher wages, pensions and health care benefits to union members. It certainly was the high water mark of labor power in America. Finally, labor had a seat at the table!

Where has it all gone?

With growing corporate power, class conflict reached new heights. The assault on labor became overwhelming, continuous, inhuman and destructive.. No wonder unions are dysfunctional and chaotic. So are most of their leaders. If they're not coerced, co-opted or corrupted, they're framed, jailed or neutralized in some way.

Only when capitalism is in the throes of crisis, deep depression and near collapse can strong labor leaders emerge. Must we relive the 1930's?

Maybe our two presidential candidates, believers in change, will come up with something better than Bush's economic stimulus package to save our collapsing economy—like repeal of the Taft-Hartley Act, the epitome of anti-labor legislation. Or enforcement of the Wagner Act (which is still on the books) that guarantees workers the right of collective bargaining, a product of Roosevelt's New Deal that raised the standard of living of the middle and working classes.

Where do the candidates stand on these issues? I haven't heard any meaningful discussion of how to save our economy. McCain seems to be set in concrete, but Obama seems to be changing the change we can believe in since he assumed his presumptive nomination in the Democratic Party. He seems to have adopted the Bill Clinton strategy of triangulation. Go after those shaky votes on the right! It worked for Bill; maybe it will work for him. There's been a sea change, lately, in Barack's change we can believe in.

Can you imagine Obama supporting Bush's intelligence surveillance law?

Well, he says he will when the compromise FISA bill comes to the Senate, granting immunity to the telecommunications corporations for their participation in warrantless wiretapping programs. So far, there are 40 lawsuits against them alleging privacy invasion.

The latest Obama glitch—his adoption of the Bush faith-based initiatives. Is he going for the evangelical vote? One of the essential principles of this democracy, I always thought, was separation of church and state. Religious charities are well and good, but isn't it the responsibility of the state to look after the welfare of its people?

End the war in Iraq? Obama says he is against the war. Cindy Sheehan, who lost her son, Casey, in the war, was hoping Barack would say "Troops out now!"

But we haven't heard anything like that from him. Each year, since 2005, we've heard a different plan. Now, he says he "will remove one to two combat brigades each month, and have all of our combat brigades out of Iraq within sixteen months…" and, of course, some will have to remain to protect our embassy and diplomats and – er – man our "impermanent bases" in the country that we will occupy permanently.

We won't go into Obama's other flip-flops. It's too painful. They are amply covered, even in the mainstream media.

So who are you going to vote for?

There are other candidates, you know, although you would never suspect it from reading or listening to the mainstream media.

There's Cynthia McKinney, Congresswoman from Georgia's 11th District, candidate for President on the Green Party ticket.

There's Bob Barr, also from Georgia, a former Congressman from the 7th District, the Libertarian Party nominee for President.

There's Chuck Baldwin, pastor and radio talk show host, nominated by the Constitution Party.

And, of course, there's Ralph Nader, who chose to run, this year, as an Independent.

If you vote for any one of these, people will say you're throwing away your vote.

Let them say it. They will be giving their votes to the corporate oligarchy.

Vote your conscience. Vote your hopes, not your fears.

You don't want to walk out of that voting booth with a grimace on your face, after holding your nose and once again voting for the lesser of two evils.

You want to walk out of there feeling good about yourself, holding your head high knowing that you exercised your first amendment rights— freedom of speech, and of the press and your right to freely assemble.

Good luck and God Bless America!

Which Side Are You On?

Is Barack Obama a social democrat or a capitalist tool?

Is John McCain a Glory Boy or a POW songbird?

If these are the choices we have in the upcoming presidential election, a faked out war hero, pushing the Bush agenda, and a corporate tool talking like a social democrat, you've got to know this country is up the creek or down the shaft.

If Barack Obama is a social democrat (read neoliberal), talking Universal Health Care but meaning Chicago School of Economics and going ga-ga over markets, you know there'll be no singer payer health plan in his, or our, future.

Obama's association with the Milton Friedman "gang of four" tells the story—receiving advice or campaign financing from Austan Goolsbee, a University of Chicago economist, billionaire Kevin Griffin, CEO of the hedge fund Citadel Investment Group, Robert Rubin, former Goldman-Sachs chief, and the Crown family of General Dynamics.

The tip-off, if any further confirmation is needed, was the speed with which Obama raced to the obligatory appearance before the Israel

Lobby (AIPAC) and groveled as no candidate ever has before, even giving Jerusalem to Israel undivided, a thorn in the peace process that has kept the Palestinians at bay for 40 years. Moreover, Obama said he will do everything in his power to prevent Iran from obtaining a nuclear weapon. Everything! Did that include bombing Iran?

This is nothing new in American politics. There has always been more fiction than fact in the run-up to national elections.

This is a country born in genocide (the Native Americans), grew up in slavery (the Africans), and finally arrived into the capitalist era with the emancipation and the Civil War. I guess it's a truism that war enhances corporate profits, the mother's milk of capitalism, as it's doing in Iraq, today.

To make it all work, capitalism has to have a tweedledum and a tweedledee—two faces, one smiling, one grim, and they can swing between one and the other, depending on the temper of the times.

We've just come through eight years of the grim face (the Bush administration and his war on terror) and now, with Bush's popularity down in the muck (below 30%), the oligarchy is looking for a smiling face. It certainly can't be McCain's, joined at the hip with George Bush, as he is, with his love of the Iraq war and tax cuts for the rich.

With 70% or more of the American people against both, it is now time for the smiling face. So, they say, let's create our ideal candidate. And so they did. They didn't mind swinging to the Democratic Party, the party that traditionally plays the "chump" role.

They chose Obama, the perfect black sheep, in looks, demeanor and intelligence, to lead the liberal elite down the garden path. Like the Pied Piper of Hamelin he also got lots of the kids behind him.

Well educated, with degrees from Columbia University and Harvard Law School, Obama went into politics and in short order became junior

United States Senator from Illinois after a stint in the Illinois Senate. He grabbed the oligarchy's attention when he delivered the keynote address at the Democratic National Convention in July 2004. He was their man!

Is it all as calculated and crafted as that? Yes, it is. Just look at the facts. Isn't it as clear as the fable of John McCain's war heroism?

It's astounding how this man, John Sidney McCain III, could become a US Senator and a presidential candidate with the amount of credible evidence proving him to be, at best, a collaborator, at worst, a traitor, while he was a POW in North Vietnam during that ill-fated war.

Where was the Pentagon? Where was the government? Where was the media? Who has investigated the allegations?

McCain was routinely bombing Hanoi from an aircraft carrier in the South China Sea. On October 26, 1967, a surface-to-air missile knocked a wing off his jet. His plane splashed into Truc Bach Lake. A compassionate Vietnamese dragged him out of the water and saved McCain's life. He was taken to a POW camp.

What actually happened to McCain in his POW camp? Was it abuse, as he claims, or was it, in fact, that he collaborated and had to cover up?

Fellow prisoners of war, Ted Guy and Gordon "Swede" Larson, have provided eye-witness accounts of McCain's treatment by his captors.

"My only contention with the McCain deal," Larson told the Phoenix New Times, "is that while he was at "The Plantation" (POW camp), to the best of my knowledge and Ted's knowledge, he was not physically abused in any way."

Another source is John McCain himself who has confessed that after three or four days after his capture, he cracked. He promised his Vietnamese captors, "I'll give you military information if you will take me to the hospital."

His captors soon realized that McCain came from a high-level naval family, his father and grandfather, admirals in the US Navy. While John III was being held captive, his father, Admiral John McCain, Jr. was in charge of all US forces in the Pacific, including those fighting in Vietnam. Any wonder then that John III was taken to a hospital reserved for Vietnamese officers, and received care from a Soviet doctor?

McCain was released in 1973, and claims to having been tortured by his North Vietnamese captors, and so the myth of the McCain war heroism began.

Now, we have those two, Obama, McCain, as our only choices for President of the United States. Which of the lesser of the two evils will you vote for?

Where is Ralph Nader now that we really need him?

Slouching Toward a Population Die-Back

⌒∿⌒

Is there a famine in our future?

When we start putting food in our gas tanks, we know Americans would rather drive than live.

"We're having a world-wide food crisis," murmured the New York Times. The rest of the media took their cue, as they usually do, and headlined the new event.

The Los Angeles Times put it this way, "Vegetable oil isn't a crime—is it? Diesel owners who switch to cooking grease can run afoul of the law. Just ask the governor." The state wants its tax on alternative fuels just as they get it from the sale of gasoline.

Drivers, in all the esoteric places, are converting their cars to run on used cooking and frying oil. Some restaurants that once found it a burden to dispose of used fry-oil are now thinking of charging for it.

But, of course, the 800 lb gorilla in the world is Ethanol.

The fear of oil peaking has caused a stampede of biofuel production across the world in the frantic search for a substitute.

As Wikipedia defines it, "Biofuel is a solid, liquid or gas fuel derived from recently dead biological material, most commonly plants... distinguishing it from fossil fuel, derived from long dead biological material."

Brazil is currently the world's leader in ethanol production. The chippie is sugarcane. It grows like topsy in that part of the world. Imperial systems were founded on it. Sugar and rum were the chief exports from the Caribbean and South America to Europe during the colonial period. Every sailor on the slave ships that plied the Atlantic to the Americas had his ration of rum.

In the United States, ethanol is made principally from corn. Its development has been a bonanza for the American corn conglomerates. The largest producer of ethanol in the U.S. is the Archer Daniels Midland Company (ADM) that touted itself, for years, as "Supermarket to the World" in TV ads.

ADM is an agricultural giant. It has made profits of $10.98 billion in 2006, and operates in North America, South America, Europe, Middle East, Africa, Asia and Pacific Rim. The company has a transportation network that circles the world capable of delivering ethanol just about anywhere.

Included in the agribusiness cabal is Monsanto reporting a net income this year that more than doubled the earnings in 2007, from $543 million to $1.12 billion.

The earnings of Cargill, another cabal member, soared by 86 % from $553 million to $1.03 billion in one year.

Any wonder, the cost of food, everywhere, is going through the roof?

Staples like wheat, rice, corn and beans, what most of the people of the third world (and other world's, too) live on, are out of reach for many. As of March this year, wheat and maize prices were 130 and 30 percent higher, respectively, than a year earlier. Rice prices have more than doubled since late January

The food price index of the U.N. Food and Agriculture Organization rose by 9 percent in 2006 and 23 percent in 2007. While millions are being driven toward starvation, giant agribusinesses are enjoying soaring earnings and profits.

In typical corporate style, with no concern for the lives of people, speculators have turned the growing worldwide food shortages into a gold mine.

"The corn-to-alcohol scheme may well be the largest single financial crime of all time," says Global Research, an educational think-tank, "Its cost to consumers in higher food prices will exceed the total cost of the so-called war in Iraq, plus the cost of escalated oil prices. There cannot be a bigger issue than food. No problem in America comes close to it in importance, because no one can escape depending on food for survival -- and we are talking about doubling or tripling the cost of basic grain commodities on which the non-rich survive."

Cars should be powered by energy from the sun or hydrogen—not food grains. The elegant process of plant creation by photosynthesis should be reserved for humanity and the other animals that walk the earth.

We can go back to the theories of Thomas Malthus, 19th Century English demographer and political economist. He opined that the number of people the earth can sustain depends on the amount of food that can be grown. Sooner or later, it will simply be impossible to feed all the people and there will be mass starvation. Malthusians continue to warn that the disaster is almost upon us.

Is there an answer for this? Sure there is. Tax the agribusiness giants instead of subsidizing them.

Subsidies began with the Agricultural Adjustment Act of 1933, in the depth of the Great Depression. It was Franklin D. Roosevelt's attempt, through the New Deal, to save the family farm by paying poor farmers not to raise crops thereby stabilizing food prices that were falling through the floor.

Through the decades, the small farmers were pushed out and the specter of corporate farming haunted America. Today, the family farm is all but gone, corporate agribusiness is aggressively robust and the subsidies are still there!

Every year, when the Farm Bill, now reaching into $300 billion, comes up for debate, the members of Congress make a Faustian deal. Those from non-farm states will vote for the subsidies if the farm state members vote for food stamps and other benefits for the poor thrown into the bill. The President usually vetoes it and we wind up with a pot pourri.

Meanwhile, food riots are breaking out across the globe from Bangladesh to Burkina Faso, from China to Cameroon, and from Uzbekistan to the United Arab Emirates.

"What we are seeing is unprecedented," says Catholic Relief Services food aid expert Lisa Kuennen-Asfaw. "If immediate needs are not met, and if resources and policies supporting increased agricultural production are not put in place soon, we are heading for a cascade of hunger the world over."

Have a good day.

On the Eve of Destruction

(with apologies to Barry McGuire)

⌒⁓⌒

**"The eastern world it tis explodin',
violence flarin', bullets loadin' …"**

The surge in Iraq is working, says George W. Bush through his military mouthpiece, General David H. Petraeus, at recent Congressional hearings. The war goes on and Iraqis (and US GIs) are being killed daily although polls show the American people never wanted this war and want their troops out now.

The presidential candidates for both parties in the 2008 election—McCain, Clinton, Obama—are proposing timetables for troop withdrawal, anywhere from six months to one hundred years. No one has yet come up with a reason why we're there, or a definition of victory, for that matter. To prevent chaos and bring democracy to the Middle East just doesn't cut it.

In any war of occupation, if the occupied nation has strong leaders who are willing to unite and lead their people into a fight, they will eventually win.

You can safely wager that long before the 100 years are up, if we don't willingly withdraw, the remnants of US forces in Iraq are likely to be evacuated from the roof of the American embassy building in Baghdad's green zone by helicopter. When the Sunnis and the Kurds and the various

Shia factions and militias get together, that will be the end of the little al-Maliki puppet government in Baghdad and the destruction of US power in Iraq; as happened in Vietnam when the Viet Cong and the Viet Minh came together in the Tet offensive and as happened to the French in Algeria when the resistance poured out of the Casbah in a great human wave…

"…but you tell me over and over and over again my friend, ah, you don't believe we're on the eve of destruction…"

Economists, across the board, are telling us we're heading into a recession, if we aren't already in one; and some say we'll be going deeper, into a depression. Well, what do you know? A war and a depression at the same time! In capitalist societies, war is frequently the antidote to depression; the cure worse than the malady. These days, economies are linked worldwide. Is there a world economic collapse in our future? Does anyone really know?

We know about the sub-prime mortgage disaster, the credit card crunch, the bail-out of Bear Stearns with taxpayer money and others yet to come (socialism for the capitalists) and things of that sort. And we've been hearing of mass layoffs of workers in manufacturing and service industries. Who needs a working class? The good paying jobs are mostly gone with the off-shoring and outsourcing of the hardware (factories) and the software (workers).

A free market system cannot exist without the purchasing power of the working class. But we've done away with all that; smashed the union movement that once gave trade unionists a living wage. We have to import the very commodities we used to make and pay more for them—unless you can shop at Walmart that has an inside track to cheap.

The government has been cooking the books for years. It's been standard procedure. One administration after another has been addicted to "la vie en rose".

We have three fundamental measurements on which we determine the state of our economy—the monthly Consumer Price Index (CPI), an indicator of inflation—the quarterly Gross Domestic Product (GDP), which tracks the economy's overall growth—and the monthly unemployment figure, an indicator of economic health. These statistics are vital to obtain a true picture of the economy. Important decisions for government and business depend on their accuracy.

Kevin Phillips, a noted commentator on economic issues and a former Republican Party strategist, charges, in the current issue of Harper's Magazine (May '08), that the economy is worse than we know, and he is able to make those charges stick.

"Since the 1960s," he says, "Washington has been forced to gull its citizens and creditors by debasing official statistics: the vital instruments with which the vigor and muscle of the American economy are measured."

"How much angrier would the electorate be," Phillips asks. "if the media, over the past five years, had been citing 8 percent unemployment (instead of 5 percent), 5 percent inflation (instead of 2 percent) and average annual growth in the 1 percent range (instead of the 3-4 percent range) … the corruption has tainted the very measures that most shape public perception of the economy."

How much longer can this system survive playing those games, plunging its head in the sand and letting the lies roll over. We've built a world of distraction in the media, in academia, in arts and entertainment; in the gross distortions we call "news" to hide it all.

The ice caps are melting, the honey bees are dying, the oil is depleting, and food is being raised to go into your gas tank. And for the Bush Administration, life is just a bowl of cherries…

**"…the pounding of the drums, the pride and disgrace,
you can bury your dead, but don't leave a trace,
hate your next-door-neighbor, but don't forget to say grace.
and you tell me over and over and over and over again my friend,
ah, you don't believe we're on the eve of destruction."**

Fundamentals

Let's get down to fundamentals.

The two warring Democratic candidates in the presidential election have their slogans.

Obama wants change. Hillary wants solutions. Yes, they discuss all the issues that are fit to discuss. Even McCain talks about death and taxes.

But nobody wants to take on the fundamentals—the source of the status quo requiring change and the root cause of the problems for which Hillary wants solutions. It's not just the economy, Stupid! It's the system...to use a Clintonian euphemism.

A system based on greed, profit and exploitation of one class by another will eventually land it in the ditch. You don't need Karl Marx to tell you that. He made a landmark analysis of Capitalism in the 19th Century and so far his predictions have been right on the money. Empires fall—from the Roman to the German. They dig their own graves.

Capitalism, by its name and nature supports the rich, propertied and corporate class. You don't have to be a rocket scientist or a Marxist to

175

see that. Competition between corporate entities, in various nations, leads to monopoly and war. When corporations control a government, it's Corporatism. We're in that stage of capitalism right now. Benito Mussolini, pre-World War II dictator of Italy, gave it a name. He called it Fascism.

For the capitalist system to survive—it must have constant economic growth and find new markets and sources of raw materials.

There are two ways to do this, the first, by going into countries, anywhere in the world, and taking what you want by military means (commerce follows the flag, as the British used to say), or it can be done by diplomacy and economic penetration. The North American Free Trade Agreement (NAFTA) is an example of the second way, the war and occupation of Iraq, an example of the first. Of course, the natives of those countries don't like either method. So, one way or another, they fight back.

Right now, we're spilling blood for oil and heading into a recession at the same time. We have a new complication that ranks with global warming. Oil is peaking. Supplies can only diminish from here on. Are we going to fight for the last drop of oil on earth before putting maximum effort into looking for alternative forms of energy? Looks that way. Big oil still has clout.

Wealth produced by the working people of this country flows in only one direction, up. According to University of California statistics, the top 1% of Americans own 33.4% of the wealth while the bottom 80%, the overwhelming majority of wage and salaried workers, are left with a measly 16%.

Do the presidential candidates discuss any of this, and if not, why not?

The answer to that is easy. They're all corporate candidates. The oligarchy can't lose, whoever is elected. The American mainstream media, that molds popular perception, supports one or another of the corporate candidates. And why not? The same corporate entities own the mainstream media. So keep the public distracted by endlessly debating the fine points of their choice, turning it into an entertaining horse race. The average Joe would do better going to the track.

The presidential candidates are fighting for the votes of "We the people…"

So why isn't it fair game to take on some of the faults and flaws of the capitalist system? Many of Obama's needs for change and Hillary's solutions to problems stem from capital's depredations. But no candidate dares to mention the "C" word.

It was not always thus. In the depth of the last depression, Roosevelt saved capitalism with the New Deal—the NRA, the WPA, the TVA and the rest of FDR's acronyms. Of course, the beginning of World War II helped. War frequently pulls capitalism's chestnuts out of the fire.

But, in 1935, the National Labor Relations Act (the Wagner Act) was passed. This put government on the spot. It had to support the working class. Government supported unionization and collective bargaining that helped distribute the wealth more equitably. So, you see, workers rights can be protected even under capitalism. All it needs is a president and an administration to fight off the economic royalists.

If that doesn't happen, there can be trouble in River City. Times change and conditions have a way of turning into their opposite. Marx's historical materialism demonstrates that. There are nodal points in history, when quantitative changes leap to a qualitative change. Revolution is such a nodal point. All phenomena in the universe consist of "matter in motion"; all things are interdependent and interconnected.

We're headed into the great unknown right now. Most economists agree a recession looms. Some pessimists see a deeper recession, some a depression rivaling that of the 1930s.

There are all kinds of ideas out there lying dormant. If understood more universally, they could be helpful in advancing the welfare of this country.

Why don't our presidential candidates talk about them? Stand up to their corporate sponsors.

Where Have All the Profits Gone?

The stock market has been bouncing around like a yo-yo on steroids.

The term "subprime" that most of us hadn't heard before, has become a household word.

Household mortgages have been avalanching and foreclosures piling up. Banks are locked in a credit crunch.

Bear Stearns, one of Wall Street's biggies, had to be bailed out by the Fed.

Banks, like bookies of yore, are laying off bad bets. The government is dancing as fast as it can, printing $600 checks to send out to everybody, hopefully creating some purchasing power for people to go out and buy stuff.

Yet, despite the stimulus package, and other fables being told by George W. Bush, reputable economists and dour newsmen are predicting a deep and long recession ahead.

According to Wikipedia, the internet encyclopedia, a recession is a decline in a country's gross domestic product for two or more successive quarters. Recessions may be associated with falling prices, called deflation, or rising prices, called inflation, in a process known as stagflation.

A severe or long recession is referred to as an economic depression. A devastating breakdown of an economy is called economic collapse.

Is that where we're headed?

It's got to be somebody's fault. Who are the villains of the piece? Capitalists? No. Entrepreneurs? No. The working class? Well, maybe.

It's the profit motive, Stupid! In the end, you know, every crook gets caught.

Where does profit come from? That is the question.

It took Karl Heinrich Marx (1818-1883) Prussian philosopher, political economist and revolutionary, to find out where profit came from. It was a discovery that ranked with Sir Isaac Newton's discovery of universal gravitation and the three laws of motion, Charles Darwin's theory of evolution and Sigmund Freud's ego, super-ego and the id.

Profit, Marx found out, is the gain capitalists receive by paying workers less than the full value of their labor. It's called "exploitation" of one class by another—an inherent feature and key element of capitalism and free markets.

What! This whole capitalist system that has taken over the world is based on out-and-out thievery! The capitalist steals the surplus value of the labor the worker puts into the commodity being produced! What a discovery!

Well, it's better than slavery where the slave owner stole 100% of the slave's labor power, except for what it cost to keep the slave alive. It's also better than feudalism where the serf was allowed to keep only about 50% of his produce, while the feudal lord took the rest for allowing the serf to work on his land. It was called share-cropping in this country and continued for quite a while after slavery was abolished in 1865. So some progress has been made.

Another landmark discovery of Marx and his collaborator, Frederick Engels, was the concept of the "class struggle". As expressed in the "Communist Manifesto", "the history of all hitherto existing society is the history of 'class struggles'"

Marx believed that capitalism, like previous economic systems will lead to its own destruction. Capitalism cuts from under its own feet the very foundation on which it produces and appropriates products. What it creates, in the process, is its own grave-diggers.

Just as capitalism replaced feudalism, capitalism, itself, will be replaced by another form, be it communism or some form of socialism allowing for a public and private sector in the economy.

There were few parts of the world which were not significantly touched by Marxist ideas in the course of the twentieth century.

Of course, the most prominent of these was Russia and the Bolshevik Revolution which led to the formation of the Union of Soviet Socialist Republics (the USSR). We don't mind talking about that. You've got to look at these things in the long sweep of history. It took capitalism a couple of hundred years to shake itself out. Since the Industrial Revolution in England, in the late 1700s, there have been many panics, booms and busts and experimentation. Capitalism leads to monopoly and war and today we're in the stage of empire building and globalization.

Now, new forms of socialism are taking the world stage. The Soviet Union was a failed experiment. China seemed to be using revisionist Marxism to transform itself from communism to a new form of aggressive capitalism, Cuba is continuing in the old tradition with Castro and his brother Raul barely keeping the old form of classical Marxism alive. But there is a new wind blowing over Latin America, with Hugo Chavez in Venezuela and socialist ferment in the rest of the South American continent.

The United States today is reaching a stage of critical mass. With an un-winnable war in Iraq costing an estimated 3 trillion dollars of borrowed money, an infrastructure showing signs of wear, a wobbly stock market, a bloated defense budget and a military force falling apart and Congress authorizing tax cuts for the rich, isn't it time we considered making some changes in our economic system before changes are thrust upon us?

George W. Bush and the US capitalist oligarchy calling the shots must be a part of the grave-digging team.

"It Smells of Sulfur"

⟨⟩

The FARC— the Revolutionary Armed Forces of Colombia—is in the news, again.

The FARC has been a thorn in the side of the Colombian government since the 1960s when it was organized after a period of political violence in the country called "La Violencia".

The organization has grown stronger since those days and now is considered to be a terrorist, Marxist, guerrilla group threatening the Colombian government. It is accused of financing its activities through cocaine trafficking and kidnappings.

This week, the Colombian military invaded Ecuadorian territory and killed Raúl Reyes, FARC's international spokesman and considered to be FARC's second-in-command. In this operation, at least 24 guerrillas were killed. It is believed that Raúl Reyes was in Ecuador negotiating the release of some kidnap victims they had been holding, including former presidential candidate Ingrid Betancourt.

The action led to a breakdown in diplomatic relations between Ecuador and Colombia, and between Venezuela and Colombia. Both Ecuador and Venezuela massed troops on the southern and northern borders of Colombia and for a while it looked grim.

President Hugo Chávez of Venezuela, who called George W. Bush "the devil" at the UN General Assembly in 2006, and said the podium still smelled of sulfur after Bush spoke there, claimed that Colombian policies are made in Washington.

The US is hip deep in this mess since it has taken the Colombian government under its wing in 1999 with what has been called "Plan Colombia"—a way to give the Colombian government $1.3 billion dollar a year to fight the war on drugs, the lion's share of which goes to the Colombian army to fight the FARC guerrillas.

Somebody got the bright idea, probably the Monsanto Company, the world's leading producer of the herbicide glyphosate, marketed as "Roundup", that by fumigating the coca plants with this herbicide, they could stop the flow of cocaine into the United States.

The glyphosate spray not only kills the coca plants but also just about everything else growing around them including agricultural crops. There is evidence that the spray causes lesions and other ill effects in children and adults. It was a boon, of course, for Monsanto, but did little to alter the price of cocaine on the streets of America.

Coca plants are not immune from the economic laws of supply and demand. If the supply of coca leaves goes down, the price of cocaine, across the world, goes up. Enterprising entrepreneurs rush into the market, disperse and grow more coca to take advantage of the higher price. This has been the experience of coca spraying for the past thirty years. There is more coca being grown in more places than ever before.

I went to Colombia, a few years back, as a member of a human rights delegation sponsored by the Colombia Support Network of Madison,

Wisconsin, to investigate the effect of fumigation on the farmers or *campesinos* where the spraying was taking place.

In the southern province of Putumayo, where the heaviest concentration of coca is grown and where the FARC is strong, we interviewed dozens of *campesinos* and *compesino* leaders. We saw the devastation of the countryside caused by the fumigation and saw the effects of the spray on children and adults in the region.

Back in Bogotá, we went to the US Embassy to show our evidence to then US Ambassador to Colombia, Anne Patterson. At the meeting, we showed the Ambassador a flyer put out by the US Department of State telling the people of Putumayo that "Roundup" was perfectly harmless to one's health. Wasn't this flagrantly misinforming the Colombian people? The question wasn't answered but an extensive dialogue ensued about the relative toxicity of the various chemicals involved. Dueling scientists had divergent opinions on the subject. It brought to mind the debate that raged over the use of Agent Orange in Vietnam.

The Ambassador's bottom line was that US drug policy aimed to reduce the amount of cocaine smuggled into the US by cutting down the amount of coca leaves grown. Also, a standard answer, "We were invited in by the Colombian government to do this."

Feeling ran high at meetings of the Organization of American States (OAS) in regard to the current crisis caused by Colombia's violation of Ecuadorian sovereignty last Saturday.

Ecuador's President, Rafael Correa, said the killing of the rebel leader may have ruined chances for the release of 12 hostages held by his rebel group. Ecuador's Foreign Minister, Maria Isabel Salvador, said that Colombia's apology for the incursion was insufficient and that the organization should send a special commission to investigate.

The Los Angeles Times reports that a US intelligence official in Washington said he could not confirm reports that American spies had tipped off the Colombian authorities that Raúl Reyes was using a satellite telephone that allowed him to be tracked.

Only George W. Bush rushed to the defense of his only ally in Latin America. On Tuesday, Bush told reporters that he telephoned Colombia's president, Alvaro Uribe, and told him that "America fully supports Colombia's democracy, and that we firmly oppose any acts of aggression that could destabilize the region."

By Wednesday, the OAS approved a resolution declaring the military raid into Ecuador a violation of sovereignty in a move aimed at easing a diplomatic and military crisis.

The resolution was approved in Washington after talks in which the United States was the hemisphere's only nation explicitly supporting Colombia.

You could smell the sulfur.

Explaining Democracy

~~

But, Son, the oligarchy always hedges its bets.

It looks very democratic because a black man and a white woman are running for president. The oligarchy has three dogs in the fight this election, with John McCain on the Republican side. But remember, all have the same master. The oligarchy likes to pick the candidate that has the most credibility with the public, yet is committed to carrying out the oligarch's agenda. That's why they hold these primaries, caucuses and elections. Keeps up appearances.

No, no, you don't understand. This is not just a democracy. This is a capitalist democracy. Our founding fathers set it up this way. Of course, back in 1776 and 1789, when we had our revolution, kicked out the British and the nation was formed, capitalism was young. The Industrial Revolution had just taken hold—a revolution on steroids.

"Malversation and peculation were rife," said Shakespeare referring to another period in history similar to this one. Exploitation was the name of the game.

We had slavery in this country until the 1880s. The Civil War was fought over differences between North and South in their economic relationships with England, the mother country. Slavery was not the issue. It was a victim of collateral damage.

"...this government cannot endure ... half slave and half free", said Lincoln.

The victory of the North ended the slave system because of its inefficiency, not for humanitarian considerations, the Abolitionists notwithstanding.

Once the nation had rid itself of the slave system, the burgeoning, ravenous new capitalists instituted a wage slave and profit system.

What does that have to do with what's happening now? Well, everything. I call it a "wage slave" system because only a part of a worker's labor is stolen from him—the surplus value he creates by his labor, over and above the value he puts into the commodity for which he is paid. That's where profit comes from. Karl Marx figured that one out but most of these capitalist economists, today, keep mum about that. It would blow their whole schtick.

You still don't get it? Well, what I am telling you is that capitalism has grown up. It's no longer a system of simple commodity production. We've gone through the market fluctuations, booms and busts, inflation and deflation, recessions and depressions, for more that 150 years. Capitalism has to grow or die. We're still growing. We're now in the period of monopoly capitalism and war is our modus operandi. We have to keep a war economy going. A domestic economy, alone, will no longer cut the mustard. That would mean social programs for the people; repeal of tax cuts for the rich. We can't countenance that. We'll simply have to go abroad to make ends meet. It's only imperialism. It's been done many times by many countries for many centuries. We have to save those places by taking over their markets and their resources—as we're doing in Iraq right now.

Why don't the people do something about it?

That's a good question. You have to understand, people are placid. They don't like to rock the boat. They can be made to act like sheep, herded this way and that, and let me tell you how. The Fourth Estate.

The Fourth Estate? That's just a fancy name for the press or what we now call the media—newspapers, magazines, radio and television, and all those honorable ways to keep the people informed. The media is also there to keep the government honest.

You call it a crock, do you? Now wait a minute. That's what the Fourth Estate is supposed to do—not what it really does. The mainstream media (MMS) is asleep at the switch. But they're not really asleep. They've just been brainwashed, co-opted, whatever you want to call it—taken over by the Second Estate.

What's the Second Estate? The nobility. We call them the ruling elite. The mighty corporations of America that have now become multinational. They own the media; Time Warner, Rupert Murdoch's News Corp, Disney, Viacom, Bertelsmann AG, Vivendi SA; half a dozen conglomerates that control just about everything we see, hear and read. As Noam Chomsky says, they manufacture consent, so everyone believes the same lies.

The control goes deeper than that. It permeates the whole system—from cradle to grave…even children in grade school. The curricula, the textbooks that are used. It runs through high school and academia. We're all subliminally trained to believe the same conventional wisdom. Then, there's government, all levels. The corporations control the levers of government. They own most of the politicians which is why so many of them are disrespected by the public. There are politicians and there are statesmen. I haven't seen a statesman in quite a while.

This doesn't last forever. There comes a time, a turning point, when people come alive, no longer sheep. When the system fails to provide the basic needs of life, the people change it. Sometimes peacefully. Usually not. The ruling class doesn't like to give up even some of its power. Then, the people have to take it forcefully. It's built into our Constitution. Our founding fathers had a couple of good ideas. One of them was the Declaration of Independence, especially this part:

> …all men are created equal, that they are endowed by their Creator with certain unalienable Rights, that among these are Life, Liberty and the pursuit of Happiness.—That to secure these rights, Governments are instituted among Men, deriving their just powers from the consent of the governed,—that **whenever any Form of Government becomes destructive to these ends, it is the Right of the People to alter or abolish it,** and to institute new Government…

Oh, now you get it. I knew you would, Son. It's built into your constitution.

Ralph Nader:
Monkey Wrench or Cattle Prod?

"Here we go again," murmured the old guard Democrats when Ralph Nader officially announced his candidacy for president in 2008, on Tim Russert's "Meet the Press" show, Sunday, Feb.24th .

"Nader—the spoiler," they called him since the 2000 election when Al Gore lost the presidency to George W. Bush. "It's all Nader's fault!" they cried. Nader was a good scapegoat, a good person to blame, so they wouldn't have to examine their own souls.

Yes, George W. Bush was named President. He won Florida by 537 votes. Ralph Nader got 97,488 votes in Florida. It's simple. If Nader hadn't run, Gore would have won!

Hold on! It's not as simple as that!

George W. Bush got just a little help from his friends. His brother Jeb Bush, who happened to be Governor of the State at the time, Katherine Harris, Secretary of State of Florida, in charge of election procedures, election officials in Fort Lauderdale who produced ballots that apparently were designed by Rube Goldberg and left hanging chads.

The US Commission on Civil Rights conducted an extensive investigation of irregularities during the 2000 presidential election in Florida, published in The Washington Post on June 5, 2001, said: "the most dramatic undercount in this election was the nonexistent ballots of the countless unknown eligible voters, who were wrongfully purged from the voter registration rolls, turned away from the polls, and by various other means prevented from exercising the franchise."

The Report went on to say: "The disenfranchisement of Florida's voters fell most harshly on the shoulders of African-Americans. Statewide, based upon county-level statistical estimates, African-American voters were nearly ten times more likely than white voters to have their ballots rejected in Florida."

The Commission pointed the finger at where the blame belonged: "the governor and the secretary of state, in particular, chose to simply ignore the mounting evidence that many counties were experiencing rising voter registration rates in communities with out-dated voting technology. Furthermore, they ignored the pleas of some supervisors of elections for guidance and help."

Then there was the US Supreme Court that stopped the re-counts and gave the Presidency to George W. Bush.

So, you must admit George W. Bush got just a little help from his friends. Everybody knows, today—it's the conventional wisdom—that George W. Bush stole that election.

But, as far as the old guard Democrats are concerned, their lost election is all Nader's fault. They blame him for the disastrous last seven years of the Bush Administration. They blame him for the Iraq war. (If Al Gore had been elected, it never would have happened) They blame Nader for Bush's failed economic policy, tax cuts for the rich and everything else bad that the Bush administration has done.

The two Democratic candidates talk endlessly about Universal Health Care but neither of them mentions those two little words, "single payer", the only way it can ever happen. Both are afraid of bucking the mammoth health insurance industry in this country. Maybe Nader can prod them into fighting a little harder for what they claim they want.

We know Senator Hillary Rodham Clinton is on the Armed Services Committee in the Senate and in the pocket of the defense industry, but then Barack Obama talks about increasing the military buildup instead of cutting the bloated military budget that we have. The sheepish Democrats might need a little cattle prod for moving on this issue.

Why is a discussion of corporate crime and corporate welfare off the table in this campaign, when corporatism in on the march.

Benito Mussolini, pre-World War II Italian dictator, defined the term "corporatism" as "fascism", and he should know. He coined the phrase and turned Italy into a fascist country that linked up with the Nazis.

Is that what we want here? Corporatism? We're certainly moving in that direction, if not already there. Congress is corporate occupied territory. We just don't want to face it. Maybe Ralph Nader can explain it to people who have closed minds. We dare not listen—because mainstream media has tried to make Nader into some kind of joke.

What about the "monkey wrench" effect? Will Nader be accused of blowing the election for the Democrats, again, in 2008? Lose to John McCain? It would take Houdini to do that. As Nader said to Tim Russert in the "Meet the Press" interview, "If the Democrats can't landslide the Republicans this year, they ought to just wrap up, close down, emerge in a different form. You think the American people are going to vote for a pro-war John McCain who almost gives an indication that he's the candidate for perpetual war…"

In the interview, Nader cites Solon Simmons, a professor at George Mason University, who made a study of the election shenanigans during the 2000 Florida campaign and argues that by cattle prodding Al Gore to the left with his aggressive, resolutely left-of-center rhetoric, Nader may have actually delivered more votes to the Democrats than he took away.

So much for the "monkey wrench" effect.

Tipping Point

⌒⁊⌒

"Be not afraid of greatness; some are born great, some achieve greatness, and others have greatness thrust upon them."

--William Shakespeare

I hate to paraphrase Donald Rumsfeld, who said: "You fight with the army you have, not with the army you want", but allow me this: "we work with the candidates we have, not with the candidate we'd like to have".

Barack Obama might not have been born great, might not have achieved greatness, but he's standing in a place where he may have greatness thrust upon him.

Most great leaders in world history did not spring full grown from the rib of Jove. They were molded by the confluence of historical events, unexpected circumstances and the pressure of the people behind them.

George Washington. He was caught in the maelstrom of an insurgent movement, pushed forward by the farmers and landowners of the 13 colonies to take on the British redcoats of George III and beat them with his rag-tag army of freedom fighters, much as Ho Chi Min and the Viet

Cong did in Vietnam with a guerrilla army fighting with bamboo spears against the tanks and helicopters of the American invaders.

What are the freedom fighters of Iraq doing right now?

If the Shia, the Sunni, and the Kurds could get together, instead of fighting a centuries old religious war, they'd have the American invaders out of there in a New York minute, probably by helicopter from the top of the US Embassy building in Baghdad. The Grand Ayatollah Ali Hussein al-Sistani is probably working on that right now.

Franklin Delano Roosevelt, the aristocratic former Governor of New York State had greatness thrust upon him by the Stock Market crash of 1929. Herbert Hoover and the Smoot-Hawley Tariff Act added to that greatness in the elections of 1932, plunging Roosevelt into the depth of the Great Depression when he took office in 1933. The Republican right-wing also thought tax cuts for the rich would be a good way to crawl out of the depression using a stimulus package.

As the story goes, Pelle the Conqueror, achieved greatness by learning how to speak Danish, whereas Alexander and Peter did it just by calling themselves "the Great".

Jesus Christ was born great, whereas Babe Ruth did it with his bat and Barry Bonds with his bat and a little help from a yellow submarine.

Revolutions don't come along very often but when they do they produce a lot of greatness. When Louis XVI and his wife, Marie Antoinette, were guillotined, Maximilien François Marie Isidore de Robespierre and his Jacobin friends had their moment in the sun, called the Reign of Terror. Liberté, Egalité, Fraternité did not emerge directly from the Reign of Terror, but eventually the great Napoleon Bonaparte did.

Napoleon's ambition was to conquer Europe (if not the world). In 1804, he crowned himself Emperor of France and proceeded to knock off one country after another until he got to Russia. There, the great Russian winter smothered him, as it did another would-be world conqueror a century and a half later.

We won't mention Hitler and Stalin and we'll go right to the wanna-be great George W. Bush. Now there's a man who would like to have greatness thrust upon him. If his Democratic opponents had any "cojones", any at all, even a wee bit, they would thrust him and his puppet-master the un-great Dick Cheney right out of office.

We had a president who was tossed, not too long ago, within the memory of most of us—Tricky Dick Nixon, in 1974. His high crime and misdemeanor was authorizing a second-rate burglary at the Watergate Hotel in Washington in order to steal some election campaign strategy from the office of the Democratic National Committee. Too bad. His burglars got caught red-handed. No greatness thrust upon Tricky Dick.

And we had a president, even more recently who was impeached by the House of Representatives in 1998, President Bill Clinton impeached, not for the real crimes and misdemeanors that he committed, like bombing Iraq on a regular basis for over a year; for supporting sanctions on the Iraq people that resulted in the death of more that a half million Iraqi children; for keeping in office a Secretary of State, Madeleine Albright, who said the deaths of these children were "worth it". No, he wasn't impeached for any of that.

Bill Clinton was impeached for denying that he had sexual relations with "that" woman—Monica Lewinsky, a White House intern. The US Senate didn't have the guts to put him on trial (as impeachment protocol called for) and, if found guilty, evict him from office. No greatness there.

Now, Bill Clinton is on the campaign trail, aiding his wife, Senator Hillary Rodham Clinton (Dem. New York) in her ambitious drive to become President of the United States. No greatness there but lots of Chutzpah.

The tipping point seems to have come with the Obama victory in the Wisconsin primary.

When young people come out to vote, you know the thrust of greatness is on the move.

Open Letter to Obama

You're rounding the turn, heading down the home stretch, running neck and neck with the lead horse, so don't blow it now.

You've got those super-delegates waiting in the paddock ready to snatch defeat from the jaws of victory. Your jaws. Your victory. This is your big chance, so don't blow it now.

Change is a great slogan. It's gotten you where you are. But it's been

co-oped, here and there, by other candidates, and it can't stand alone. It's a generality, or, as McCain would say a "platitude". You're got to bite the bullet and get specific. I know specificity can get you into deep do-do, but you've got to do it. Just say those two little words; they're gentle and non-aggressive. They won't bite. "Single Payer".

"Socialized Medicine!" they'll scream. And hit you with everything they've got. They'll call you a "communist", or even worse, a social democrat. They did it to Dennis Kucinich who merely murmured "single payer" and they knocked him out of the box before he even got into it.

You're a man of fortitude and can take anything they can throw at you.

You can show them that the word "socialized" doesn't scare you into submission. You can show them that "Socialized Education", made this country great. Not just grade school public education for every child, but the Land-Grant College system, for example. Every state in the Union has one as well as the territories and the District of Columbia. They were established way back in the 19th Century by the Morrill Act of 1862 and extended in 1890. Justin S. Morrill was the senior Senator from Vermont. The mission of these Acts was "to teach agriculture, military tactic, the mechanic arts, and home economics, not to the exclusion of classical studies, so that members of the working classes might obtain a practical college education".

The mission of the Land-Grant Universities was further expanded by the Hatch Act of 1887 and the Smith-Lever Act of 1914 to provide federal funds to states to establish agricultural experiment stations and cooperative extension services, the sending of agents into rural areas to help bring the result of agricultural research to the end users.

Then, after World War II, there was the GI Bill of Rights. GI, for those too young to remember, stood for "Government Issue", the returning World War II veteran. The Act paid for a GI's entire education. It encouraged universities across the country to expand enrollment. The University of Michigan, for example, had fewer than 10,000 students prior to the war. In 1948 their enrollment was well over 30,000. Syracuse University saw their enrollment skyrocket from approximately 6,000 before the war to 19,000 students in 1947.

Another provision was known as the 52–20 clause. This enabled all former servicemen to receive $20 once a week for 52 weeks a year while they were looking for work. The GI Bill applied to all who served in the armed services, including African-Americans and women.

Now, there's a social(ist) program worth emulating.

It's time to apply it to health as well as education. Most civilized countries around the world already do with univeral health care for their citizens. All we do is talk about it and try to devise schemes that fit into the profit-taking schemes of the health insurance industry. It's not going to work.

So, Barack, just say those two little words. You may have to back away from some of your supporters. Get those mammoth health insurance companies off your back. Hillary knuckled under to them. You don't have to do that. You need a landslide vote to frustrate those super-delegates. You need the people and the wind at your back to beat Hillary to the finish line and McCain to the White House. And those two little words will do it.

Remember, Barack, we've come a long way.

This country was born in genocide (the killing of the Indians) and grew up as a slaveocracy (use of the Africans). The myth that our founding fathers were liberal democrats is just that, a myth. They were rich, white, landowners (only landowners could vote) and most were also slave owners. Yes, they broke from colonialism and beat back the British. They wrote the constitution to suit their needs. But we lucked out. It was Thomas Jefferson (also a slaveholder) who put democracy into our constitution with the Bill of Rights, the first ten amendments. Ex-slaves got the vote with the 14th Amendment, ratified in 1868, women with the 19th Amendment in 1920.

It's now time to extend those rights, to guarantee health care for the American people.

You must learn to walk in the footsteps of the great Americans this country has produced; not only men like Senator Justin S. Morrill, but also unionists and political activists like Eugene V. Debs, one of the founders of the Industrial Workers of the World (IWW), organizer of one of the first industrial unions in the United States, the American

Railway Union. He ran for President of the United States five times as the Socialist Party of America candidate, in 1904, 1908, 1912, and 1920, the last time from prison where he was jailed for his part in the Pullman strike and received a million votes.

You must walk in the footsteps of the great John L. Lewis, organizer of the mine workers and the Congress of Industrial Organizations (CIO) which established the United Steel Workers of America and helped organize millions of other industrial workers in the 1930s.

And, of course, you must walk in the footsteps of Abraham Lincoln who bucked the slave system and saved the Union.

Today, the Union must be saved again, and you're the man to do it.

On the Hunt for Change

Let's cut to the chase.

What this country needs is a good 25-cent Havana cigar and a lesson in political economy.

If you can explain the Theory of Surplus Value clearly enough, you'd make a Communist out of every working class American. Stop right there! Don't go reaching for your copy of Marx's *Das Kapital!*

The question is simply this. Do you want your labor power stolen from you—or any part of the value of your labor "taken" by somebody else? That's what happens when you work for someone producing a commodity that he sells in the marketplace.

I know you're going to challenge this because you're in a union and are getting a fair wage for your work. And you keep getting raises and you feel good about it, and you love your boss, and you think you are getting paid fully for the work you do for him. Well, think again.

And the first thing you should think of is, "How is he making a profit and staying in business?" That's the rub and here is where you have to get a little help from your friend, Karl.

203

Face it—your labor is producing the boss' profit—not his factory, not his machines, not his land, not his entrepreneurial skills in the marketplace. Yes, some say he deserves a reward for risking his capital. Okay, but why should it come out of your hide? It's your labor and the labor of your fellow workers, from which surplus value is derived. And the surplus value you produce is his profit.

Marx put it this way in his theory of exploitation: "living labour is able to create and conserve more value than it costs the employer to buy; which is exactly the economic reason why the employer buys it. That's how he preserves and augments the value of the capital at his command. Thus, the surplus labour is *unpaid* labour appropriated by employers in the form of work-time. Human labor is the only source of net new economic value, and that's his profit." And it's coming out of **YOU**.

You're okay with that? Then stop reading, right now.

For those who are game to explore a little more, we can dig deeper, not only into Marx, but those economists who preceded him like Adam Smith, John Stuart Mill, David Ricardo and others, the classical economists of capitalism who came up with the concepts of "the free market" and the "invisible hand."

In 1776, Adam Smith published his great work, *An Inquiry into the Nature and Causes of the Wealth of Nations* in which he defined the transition from feudalism to the incoming capitalist system via the industrial revolution that began in late 18th Century England. He examined in detail the consequences of economic freedom, the role of self-interest, division of labor, markets and the international implications of a laissez-faire economy. He made an important contribution to the understanding of capitalism and how it worked, which Marx studied assiduously at the British Museum.

In 1867, just about a century after *Wealth of Nations*, Karl Marx published his own work, *Das Kapital*, or "Capital", in which he defined the transition from capitalism to the inevitable next stage, the incoming socialist system, where the means of production are in the hands of the society as a whole instead of owned by individuals or corporate entities.

Adam Smith tried to demonstrate how self-interest (free enterprise, rugged individualism) produces the most efficient use of resources in a nation's economy. To underscore his laissez-faire convictions, Smith argued that social control of markets are ineffectual compared to uncontrolled market forces.

Marx knocked some of Smith's theories into a cocked hat. He proved that the "free market" wasn't free and that the "invisible hand" of the market, instead of maintaining economic stability, led the system into cycles of boom and bust. The clincher was his theory of surplus value that exposed the "profit" system as the villain of the piece. Marx pointed to the entire capitalist class as an exploitative entity, and to capitalism as a system based on exploitation.

Marx said his aim was to bring scientific method to political economy and in this way "reveal the law of motion of modern society". By showing how capitalist development was the precursor of a new, socialist mode of production, he aimed to provide a scientific foundation for the modern labor movement.

Capitalism has had a pretty good run now for more than two hundred years. It's been tried and tested and what does the report card look like? Not bad, you say? Look at the goods we've produced for the welfare of the whole population.

Well, let's look at it. What you see depends on where you're standing. If you're in the belly of the beast, enjoying the fruits of stolen labor-power, it might look pretty good. But if you're one of the masses, a member of the working class struggling to keep body and soul together, one who has offered up the surplus value of your labor for your employer's profit, you might take a different view of the situation.

When you look around and see what capitalism has done to the earth and to the environment, it disgusts you further. Capitalist entrepreneurs have not only stolen part of your labor, but they've stolen the gifts of nature; the oil, the coal and other fossil fuels, the distillation of the earliest organic matter— the trees of the forest, the minerals and metals providing the wealth for man to exploit. These are not man made objects for sale or profit. They should belong to no person or entity because they belong to everyone who walks the earth, like the air they breathe and the water that supports life. (The capitalists are trying to get a corner on that, too) At the same time, while they despoil the earth with their industrial operations, they try to hand off their mess as social cost to the community as a whole.

Chief Joseph, a leader of the Nez Perce tribe in the Pacific Northwest, once said, "I think of the Earth as our Mother."

I know what you're going to say, "The Soviet Union, a supposedly socialist nation made an even bigger mess of it." Yes, they did, and so is China, now. But the key word there is "supposedly". The Soviet Union was co-oped by a dictator, Stalin, after Lenin died and Trotsky was "axed" in 1940. Socialism is still being tested in various forms, in Scandinavia, in Cuba, now in South America. Hugo Chavez in Venezuela is bringing the nation closer to what socialism is supposed to look like. Like the geologic plates in the earth, economic systems move very slowly. They only change at times of sheer necessity, when they no longer serve the masses. That's why revolutions are so hard to come by.

"All roads lead to socialism," said Marx. What's wrong with looking for a better road?

As for the Havana cigar mentioned earlier, that's to puff on while taking this lesson in political economy. Or, as Rudyard Kipling might have said, "A lesson is only a lesson, but a good cigar is a smoke."

Rescission

No, this is not about the Equal Rights Amendment and its failure because of rescission by some states. It's about the coming recession and how to ward off a potential economic collapse before the crash. Most economists agree we're heading into one.

"Firms will go to great lengths to hide or delay reporting losses," Paul Ashworth of Capital Economics told The New York Times (1/13/08), "What we know now therefore might only be the tip of the iceberg." We'd better know the whole truth now and start doing something about it.

Let's start off by rescinding the Bush tax cuts, end the wasteful war in Iraq and soak the rich. Pour the money gained into massive public works, repairing the nation's neglected infrastructure and rebuild cities blown apart by natural disasters such as Katrina. That will create more jobs than the "trickle down" system, highly touted by corporate interests that want tax cuts for themselves and their enterprises.

Another positive step would be National Health Insurance via single payer, the payer being the government; a system successfully used by industrialized nations in Europe and around the world. It would save billions in private health insurer profits and overlapping administrative costs. Opponents call it "socialized medicine". So be it. Health care, like education, should be a right and not a privilege.

The tactics of the opposition is to demonize government. They harangue the public about the evils of "big government" as though it were some kind of bogeyman. What's wrong with government? It's the instrument of "We, the People...". The only thing we have to be careful about is electing politicians that will serve our interests.

The rich would like a nice, small government that would cut entitlements for the people and allow them the giant tax cuts that they have been taking. As for military spending, the sky's the limit.

The oligarchy—that interlocking and overlapping group of corporate executives, their foundations, their think-tanks, and their political organizations and parties—runs this country. They have their hangers-on in academia and the mainstream media; otherwise known as the running dogs of capitalism.

Through their corporate eyes, the oligarchy sees the handwriting on the wall it is up against. When the economy sours and times get tough, people look around and see what's happened to them while they weren't paying attention. Resistance begins to build. It's happened many times before. It will happen again.

This time, the situation is quite different. The labor movement has been expunged. With new technology and new weapons of governance, the oligarchy has been flexing its muscles. It has learned how to induce fear in the populace, perhaps from a well-trained practitioner.

"The best political weapon is the weapon of terror. Cruelty commands respect. Men may hate us. But, we don't ask for their love; only for their fear," said Heinrich Himmler, chief of the SS in Nazi Germany.

At the risk of drawing parallels, is that where Bush got the idea for his "war on terror"? The 911 "events" happened right on time. Americans are fearful of more terrorist attacks.

That gives the Bush Administration its *raison d'être*. First you look for foreign terrorists—then you look for them at home. You prepare the ground with a Patriot Act and then surveillance without a court order. Get rid of Habeas Corpus in the meantime; and maybe prepare some local Guantanamo for American residents.

Are we going to allow fascism to creep into this country on little cats' feet? Americans are too smart for that. Corporate greed will crash the economy. You can count on that. And when it does, you will see change. Docility out. Militancy in.

Change. It seems to have become the buzz word in the presidential campaign. All the Democrats are talking about it, even some Republicans. What kind of change are they talking about? That's the chippie.

Right now, some of the Democratic candidates are talking about ending the war in Iraq, but each has a different time-table for doing it. Some talk about health care plans but none mention that dreaded term, "single payer". And there's a good reason why—campaign contributions from the health insurance industry. Some talk about tax cuts; oh yes, for the middle class.

So who do you vote for? It's like playing Russian roulette. You mark your ballot and you take your chances. It's that "lesser of two evils" choice again. You can't get away from it. Let Mike Bloomberg run as a one-man third party. At least it will give you a choice. Some choice!

"Eternal vigilance is the price of Liberty". No, it wasn't Thomas Jefferson who said that, though often attributed to him. It was Wendell Phillips, a Boston lawyer, abolitionist and advocate for Native Americans, in a speech before the Massachusetts Anti-Slavery Society in 1852.

He also said, "The hand entrusted with power becomes … the necessary enemy of the people. Only by continual oversight can the democrat in office be prevented from hardening into a despot: only by unintermitted Agitation can a people be kept sufficiently awake to principle not to let liberty be smothered in material prosperity."

Failed Policies, Failing Nation

Brother, can you spare a dime?

The illegitimate Bush Administration (product of a stolen election in the year 2000) has instituted a series of failed policies, foreign and domestic, since it took power.

As a result, the nation, today, is failing. We are heading into an economic no-man's-land on the home front and into a perilous situation in the world, the chaos spreading out from the disaster our military has created in Iraq.

Starting a war in Iraq, in March of 2003, turned into the most catastrophic foreign policy decision this country has ever made. It was based on the lie that there were weapons of mass destruction in that country that were a threat to us. Four and a half years later, we're still spending American lives and billions of taxpayer dollars as a result of that lie.

The 911 "events", George Bush's "Reichstag Fire", gave him the foothold to climb aboard the fright engine that propels the "war on terror". The phrase is a gimmick for maintaining an endless war. The pattern is clear. Scare the devil into people and you'll get away with murder – mass murder.

And so he has. Two trillion dollars later, our troops in Iraq are running around in circles chasing and killing Iraqi civilian insurgents (freedom fighters?) and our soldiers are being killed for no purpose. The word victory is meaningless. A Bush speechwriter came up with a fetching slogan, "When the Iraqis stand up, we'll stand down". Sheer, meaningless nonsense. Bush and the Pentagon neocons have no intention of pulling out of Iraq by anyone's time-table. Former DOD Secretary Donald Rumsfeld and his neocon coterie in the Pentagon made that quite clear by approving the tensile report of the William Kristol-Robert Kagan so-called educational organization, "Project for a New American Century", a bare-faced exposition of their hegemonic head trip through the Middle East, if not the world.

Supplemental funding bills, voted on by the sheeply Democrats in Congress, provide for the construction of up to 14 permanent US bases in Iraq. The idea is to use these bases to project US power throughout the Middle East and to control sources of oil as far east as the Caspian region.

We've seen the result of it thus far; the destruction of Afghanistan and Iraq and the exacerbation of a civil war in Iraq.

Failed Foreign Policy #2: Bush's unfettered support for the cagey president of Pakistan, Pervez Musharraf, to the tune of ten billion dollars.

Musharraf was supposed to use that money to help fight the "war on terror"—defeat Al Qaeda, eliminate the Taliban and capture Osama bin Laden, who reputedly has been hanging out in the tribal areas on the Afghan border. Musharraf has done none of these things.

A rational policy analyst might figure out that Musharraf has been playing a double game; using the ten billion to entrench himself in power while making token efforts to fight Al Qaeda and chase bin Laden around. Meanwhile, Islamic fundamentalists are gaining strength and are poised to take over the country, including its stockpile of nuclear weapons. With the assassination of Benazir Bhutto, who might have made a difference, the viability of Musharraf is even shakier. Nice going, George W. Bush! What do we do now?

Domestic policies haven't fared much better. Tax cuts for the rich haven't helped. The destruction of the labor movement is almost complete. With the off-shoring of manufacturing and the outsourcing of jobs, purchasing power is kicking into the dirt. The rise in the number of billionaires may be what's dragging the economy around. But without a viable middle class and with a destitute underclass, the economy won't get very far.

Economists are predicting a recession in the near future, if, in fact, it hasn't already come through the rabbit hole. This one may have a bottomless pit, and we may be staring deep depression right in the face.

Depression stares right back at you with two faces—hyperinflation and deflation. You don't know which will be the one that gets you. Hyperinflation is inflation that is out of control (Germany after World War I). Prices increase rapidly as the currency loses its value. Deflation is the opposite—a decrease in the general price level and in the money supply. There's not much around (US after the Stock Market crash of 1929).

These days we have something new. We have the Euro to fight, the currency of united Europe. With oil now at $100 a barrel, if we have to start paying for it in Euros, we'll be well on our way to hell in a hand-basket. We have China and Japan bankrolling our debt. If they should call in their paper, we will have arrived in Hades without a paddle.

Has Bush come up with any ameliorating economic policies that might stop the plunge? Not that anyone can see, hear or smell. Within the next year, the lame duck will be quacking off the stage of history, leaving young American soldiers still dying in Iraq.

"Once in khaki suits, gee we looked swell,
Full of that Yankee Doodly Dum …

Say, don't you remember, I'm your pal?
Buddy, can you spare a dime?"

The Oligarchy Has Picked Its Candidate!

The wreckage caused by the Republicans and the Bush Administration is even too much for the corporate oligarchy to take. Although Republicans have usually been their favored party, they now want a Democrat in the White House and they want that Democrat to be Hillary Clinton.

The Hillary-Bill combo has worked for the oligarchy before and will work for it again. They've been tried, tested, and vetted to carry forward the oligarch agenda. Our two-party system pays close attention to the dressing of democracy; there always has to be a choice, a Tweedledee and a Tweedledum and always a way to vote for a lesser of two evils—which, unfortunately, becomes the evil of two lessers. Through the strategy of triangulation, the Clintons have achieved the strangulation of the democratic wing of the Democratic Party. Where are you, Dick Morris, now that the Clintons need you again?

The running dogs (the fourth estate) have gotten the message and you can hear the slow build of their howl. They can stage a mighty convincing horse race. But the election is already being fixed, as it was stolen in 2000 and 2004.

That's capitalism, for you. Its nature is to show the appearance of democracy, masking the actuality of oligarchic control, while robbing the working class of the surplus value it creates. The Clintons have proven they can do the oligarchy's dirty work when called upon to do it. They will get the prize money for services rendered.

So, let's follow the money.

The Military Industrial Complex is a Member of the Oligarchy (MOTO). This year, the war industry, Lockheed Martin, Boeing, Northrop-Grumman, Raytheon and General Dynamics, to name a few, has shelled out more money to Democratic candidates than to Republicans, and Hillary has gotten the lion's share of that. The manipulators of power always hedge their bets. They play both sided against the middle.

"Mrs. Clinton has also emerged as Wall Street's favorite." says Leonard Doyle, Washington correspondent for *The Independent*, "Investment bankers have opened their wallets in unprecedented numbers for the New York senator and, in the process, dumped their earlier favorite, Barack Obama."

Big Pharma and the Health Insurance Industry (MOTO) has already socked it to 'em. Even though you never heard the words, "single payer" even whispered, back in '93 when the Clintons were faking a Universal Health Plan, the "industry" dropped Harry and Louise, characters in a TV commercial, on them that exposed their plan as a "Rube Goldberg" that would never work. Now that Hillary is running for president, she is tinkering with another *Hillarycare* plan. This time she is making sure the plan won't offend the industry. So the industry has opened its "alms" to her.

According to the California Nurses Association and the National Nurses Organizing Committee, the healthcare industry (which includes drug and insurance companies) spent more that $2.2 billion on federal lobbying over the past decade. Senator Hillary Clinton (D) and Senator John McCain (R) collected 40% of the overall total.

The Oil and Gas Industry is a major player in the Oligarchy (MOTO). Big Oil is not running on empty yet. There is still oil to be stolen around the world. But, there will be blood. Senator Hillary Clinton is the receiver of the largest largesse of Oil and Gas than any other Democrat in the presidential campaign: $151,950.00.

Iraq and Iran – a couple of delicate subjects. Hillary walks on eggs when she talks about them. Her stance must please the Oligarchy.

On October 10, 2002, she made her now famous, or infamous, speech on the Senate floor, and voted in favor of S.J. Res. 45, "A Resolution to Authorize the Use of United States Armed Forces Against Iraq" in support of Bush's war. Even more despicable, in defending her position, she subtlety implies a connection between the attack on the World Trade Towers of 9/11 and Saddam Hussein in these words, "…from the perspective of a Senator from New York who has seen all too closely the consequences of last year's terrible attacks on our nation…in balancing the risks of action versus inaction, I think New Yorkers who have gone through the fires of hell may be more attuned to the risk of not acting. I know I am."

Hawk Hillary goes even further on **Iran**. Speaking at Princeton University on the occasion of the Wilson School's 75th anniversary, last year, she must have pleased both the Oligarchy and the Israel Lobby with these words: "…a nuclear Iran is a danger to Israel, to its neighbors and beyond. The regime's pro-terrorist, anti-American and anti-Israel rhetoric only underscores the urgency of the threat it poses…*and we cannot take any option off the table* (emphasis mine).

The Kyl-Lieberman Amendment in the Senate, designating Iran's National Guard as a terrorist organization, for which Hillary voted, rests on intelligence as shaky as the claims that led us into the Iraq war and plays right into the hands of the neo-con oligarchy thirsting for another war.

So, what's the answer, campaign finance reform? We have a chicken-egg situation here. You can't get the hawks out of the nest with other hawks bought and paid for by the oligarchy.

Where is Houdini now that we really need him?

Only Pawns in the Game

You can demonize Bush and Cheney (rightfully) until hell freezes over—but it's not going to change anything. Keith Olbermann does it almost every night on his MSNBC television show, but it doesn't change anything. Trashing Bush and Cheney or Hillary or Obama might make a lot of people feel good, but it doesn't change anything. They're only pawns in the game.

The real power resides in the corporate oligarchy that runs this country. It has a strangle hold on America. The only point of an election in our two party-one party system is to determine which one carries out the agenda. If we do something about that, we might be able to change something.

David Korten, author of "*When Corporations Rule the World*", points out that "the basic design of the private-benefit corporation was created in 1600 when the British crown chartered the British East India Company as what is best described as a legalized criminal syndicate to colonize the resources and economies of distant lands..." Today's American corporations evolved from that.

When you see the feeding frenzy of US corporations in Iraq—Halliburton, Bechtel, Blackwater, and a host of others, you can understand what Korten is talking about.

The corporation is a separate legal entity having its own rights, privileges, and liabilities distinct from those of its members. The private-benefit corporation is just that—a corporation chartered for its own private benefit, but it has to provide some socially positive good. If the corporation, chartered by the state, fails to provide the function for which it is chartered, or misapplies the function, the charter can be revoked. The state giveth and the state can taketh away. But when was the last time you heard of a corporation's charter being revoked?

Over the years, the Supreme Court has bestowed additional blessings on corporations. In effect, it has made them almost human, granting them some of the same rights as US citizens, freedom of speech and freedom of the press, for example. Corporations can express there opinions in public and in the media as you or I can. This gives them enormous power, simply because they have more mullah than you or I. They can buy up commercial television time and print media ads and faux news coverage, because they have the power and the money and besides, they own most of the mainstream media.

As Sarah Stodola says in *The Brooklyn Rail*, "The Supreme Court has interpreted the Constitution in a manner that has allowed corporations to ascend to unprecedented levels of power. The phenomenon even has a name, and that name is 'corporate personhood.' And corporate personhood, friends, is why corporations are able to buy elections."

So what are we going to do to change all this?

Well, there are some things that can be done, short of revolution. We can start evaluating capitalism, for starters.

Elect a Congress that serves "We the People", not "They, the corporations". Easier said than done. How do you find candidates who are not beholden to corporations, special interests or any ethnic voting block?

I would hate to think we will have to wait for the looming economic collapse to do the job for us. We are living on borrowed time. When purchasing power of the US citizen reaches the end of its rope, the collapse will come. You can take that to the bank.

The Great Depression of the 1930s must have taught us something. When people lose everything they tend to wake up. They look around and see what's been done to them and what they've done to themselves by not paying attention. From their Hoovervilles, the people, hit by the depression, saw Hoover and his rotten administration for what it was, and threw the bums out. They elected new, progressive leaders (FDR Democrats), who saved capitalism with safety nets and a "New Deal".

Can we do something like that again; hopefully before the coming economic collapse? We'd better start trying now, and maybe ease the pain. Here are some things that need to be done.

Reverse Reaganomics. Reinstitute regulation of industry. Make the Food and Drug Administration (FDA) and the Federal Trade Commission (FTC), for example, do their jobs, so that we don't have US corporations off-shoring their manufacturing to another country, like China, for example, and then importing their product, like toys, for example, painted with lead, for our children to play with.

Soak the Rich, a phrase coined by FDR when he spoke about the "Economic Royalists" who brought this country to its knees. Instead of cutting taxes for the rich, as Bush has been doing, raise taxes for the rich and their corporate enterprises, as they did during the great depression when FDR laid a tax rate on them of over 90% in the upper brackets.

Marshal Plan on Energy -- Go cold turkey on our addiction to oil. Massive investment in the new technologies of alternative energy sources, wind, solar, geothermal. Halt the return to nuclear, and head off the development of biofuels that will put our food into your gas tanks. We can create new high-tech industries and high-paying jobs with a new energy world.

Single Payer Universal Health Care – end the merry-go-round on health care by political candidates. Get rid of the blood-sucking health insurance companies, once and for all. And make health care for our citizens a right and not a privilege. Any candidate for office will get elected on that platform.

Stop the Hemorrhaging in Afghanistan and Iraq – Four thousand dead American soldiers is four thousand too many. Two trillion dollars to destroy two countries is two trillion dollars that could have been used to rebuild the infrastructure of our country and have enough left to enhance the lives of our young and our old.

  David Korten says, "Capitalism, which means quite literally rule by financial capital—by money and those who have it—in disregard of all non-financial values, has triumphed over democracy, markets, justice, life, and spirit. There are other ways to organize human societies to actualize the positive benefits of markets and private ownership. They require strong, active, democratically accountable governments to set and enforce rules that

assure costs are internalized, equity is maintained, and market forces are channeled to the service of democracy, justice, life, and spirit."

Yes, we can do all that, if we want to.

Universal Shell Game

Talk about clout! The power of the Health Insurance Industry in the United States is staggering. If they were sent to Iraq, they'd win the war in a day.

Most of the candidates in the horse race for the 2008 presidential nomination are doing a Ring Around the Rosie, an old, fabled, nursery rhyme that dates back to the days of the bubonic plague, when a red rash ring was a symptom of the disease.

"My health care program is better than yours!" the candidates shout at each other as their campaigns ring around the nation.

The Democrats are particularly vociferous. Each claims that their plan will give the people Universal Health Insurance. Of course, all their plans are about the same, with minor differences, all feeding into the maw of the Health Insurance Industry, which we shall call HI or bubonic plague.

What are the candidates actually talking about? Listen to this! Individual mandates. That means people without health insurance will be forced to buy it. It will be compulsory, like auto insurance is for car owners. But, who will they buy it from? The health insurance companies, of course.

And if they can't afford it? Well, there's always Uncle Sam. The Democrats lay that one off on the government. If a family can't afford the insurance, the government will subsidize the family by paying part of the cost. What a bonanza for the HI, a bubonic plague for the rest of us.

There is only one, among the candidates, in either party—Dennis Kucinich, a Democrat, who has the guts to grab the tiger by the tail and use those dreaded words: SINGLE PAYER, the key words representing a true Universal Health Plan, where the government collects the taxes and is the single payer for all health services. Every civilized industrial country has such a plan. That's the very nature of the concept: "insurance". All for one. One for all. We all put money into the big pot, through premiums or taxes, call it what you will—the greater the number of participants (why not the whole country) the wider the pool, the less cost to the individual subscribers—and when we need it, we get all necessary health care services free of charge. Is that so hard to understand?

In a stroke, this would make America's health insurance industry (the most inefficient organism in the world) obsolete. What we have now is a multiplicity of employer, individual and government plans, a wilderness of paper work, sky-high administrative costs, increasing co-pays and cut-backs in care. Can't we get rid of that? Not so easy. It's a Catch 22. Don't mess with the sacred cow.

Back in 1993, in the salad days of the Clinton administration, Bill and Hillary, the Bonnie and Clyde of politics, tried to construct a government- aided health care program that would fit into the existing system, otherwise known as "a Rube Goldberg". They stirred up the hornets' nest.

Harry and Louise, a nice middle-aged couple, stars of the television commercial sponsored by the health insurance industry sat around the homey kitchen table, talking about the threat of "socialized medicine" hanging over the nation like the sword of Damocles.

Hillary got her head handed to her. She set the single payer movement back a generation. Now, she's trying it again, this time as candidate for the presidency.

Just this week, the Securities and Exchange Commission pulled back the curtain a bit so that we could get a glimpse of the mountains of loot and corruption that exists in the health insurance industry.

As reported in *The New York Times,* (12-08-07) Dr. William W. McGuire, the former chief executive of UnitedHealth Group, the largest conglomerate of health insurance companies in the country, has agreed to give back $418 million to settle claims related to back-dated stock options. He will also return $198 million to UnitedHealth shareholders. However, he will be allowed to keep stock options valued at $800 million.

"These forfeitures," says *The New York Times,* "are the first time regulators have successfully employed corporate governance rules put in place after the collapse of Enron that force executives to disgorge ill-gotten gains."

This gives you an inkling of the kind of money CEOs of health insurance companies walk away with—money that should be going into payment for your medical care.

Doctors don't like the present system any more than their patients do. For years, the American Medical Association fought pre-paid medical plans, calling them "socialized medicine", although the government had nothing to do with them. The AMA didn't anticipate the sneak attack of the insurance industry.

The health insurance companies gobbled up these pre-paid medical plans, calling them Health Maintenance Organizations (HMOs). They readily accepted Medicare and Medicaid, sopping up all that loose cash. They turned the HMOs into their opposite—not "socialized medicine" for the people but corporate welfare for the insurance companies. Through the years, they increased premiums and cut services, raking in billions in profits. The doctors allowed themselves to be co-opted and blind-sided. They allowed the pre-paid plans to get away from them. Their fear of "socialized medicine" dimmed their vision. Instead of "socialized medicine" they got privatized sweat-shops where some doctors can't make medical decisions without the approval of an HMO bureaucrat.

Health Insurance has now become a major issue in the 2008 presidential campaign. Isn't there anyone else in the campaign or in Congress, besides Dennis Kucinich, who is willing to take on this health industry behemoth?

You may find the answer to that question in the amount the health insurance industry is contributing to the campaigns of the candidates.

Homeless in Paradise

⌒γ⌒

In the United States of America, the greatest country in the world, as many as three and a half million people experience homelessness in a given year (1% of the entire US population or 10% of its poor) and of that, 1.37 million (or 39%) are children under the age of 18.

The total number of billionaires in the world is 793 with 371 of them being in the United States of America, that's about 322 more than there were 20 years ago.

If it can be said that people with money and power run the world, then 1% of America's wealthiest and most powerful run America behind a façade of democracy. The façade is coming apart and the true nature of this government is plain to see.

After four years of a useless war, costing Americans their lives and treasury, and enriching the multitude of corporate entities slurping up billions at the Iraqi trough, we have allowed the new robber barons, Bush and his crony capitalist friends to continue conning us out of house and home, our country. Our constitution is in shreds and our economy is about to crash. Don't let any of the Wall Street freaks try to fool you. They're as scared as we are.

What happens when an economic system reaches the end of its days; when purchasing power dries up and workers can no longer buy the products they produce?

When Capitalism still had some vigor, Henry Ford said he would price his cars so that his workers could afford to buy them.

Do you find that kind of insight in Corporate America today? Not on your life! First, they break the unions and then they outsource their high-paying manufacturing jobs. It's a race to the bottom. Go to wherever the lowest wages can be found. All we get to hear is that giant sucking sound that Ross Perot talked about when he was running for president – American good paying jobs and manufacturing plants leaving the country.

Let's call it "globalization." Some economists, like Milton Friedman, say "oh, well, that's capitalism".

I hate to sound like an old-time Trotskyite, but I'm beginning to believe now that our political and economic system will have to get worse, before it can get better. We're going to have to take some "shock and awe" in this country to knock some of the lethargy out of our citizens, brainwashed by the corporate media. And it's not just the media. The almost deliberate act of dumbing down the populous has been built into the fabric of society—from public education to academia to computer games. To keep the sheep compliant, I presume.

When was the last time you heard the labor theories of value or the theory of surplus value discussed anywhere in the public media? The best they can do is give us Brittany Spears and O.J. Simpson.

You wouldn't know, from what you learned in school or read in the papers, that Franklin D Roosevelt, when he became president in the depth of the depression in 1933, saved capitalism by providing a "safety net" for the millions of destitute Americans. He did it with the NRA,

WPA. TWA, CCC, AAA, Social Security and other "socialist-like" programs such as Aid to Families with Dependent Children.

So where have all the alphabets gone—along with the flowers of the "new left" of the 1960s? We thought they'd re-descend in the 1990s, but they haven't shown up yet.

So I think it's a matter of taking things into our own hands. We have a line-up of presidential candidates, Republicans and Democrats, most of them in the pockets of corporate interests, who will take us back to the same old stand, except, perhaps for Republican Ron Paul and Democrat Dennis Kucinich. But they have already been ruled out of the running because they have something helpful to say to the American people. Not allowed.

Now, Democratic candidate, Joe Biden, has just announced that he will move to impeach President Bush if he bombs Iran. Isn't that courageous! Doesn't Joe have enough evidence of high crimes and misdemeanors right now and hasn't he had them for the last three or four years; enough to move those proceedings from the Senate which he can't because impeachment must originate in the House of Representatives. Joe must know that. But he needs something to grandstand on while running for president. This is typical of the kind of tactics candidates like to use in futzing with the minds of the voters.

It appears that matters are coming to a head, building toward the perfect storm. With the sub-prime mortgage disaster, a dismal forecast in consumer spending, the maxing out of credit cards and the Fed fighting the credit crunch, can a recession be far behind? We might be lucky if it's only a recession. We could get the kind of economic collapse that would make the last depression look like a tea party. With friends like China, who needs enemies? We've fought this Iraqi war (which we're still fighting) on the cuff—about two trillion dollars worth. China, a prime creditor, could call in some of this debt if they wanted to be mean.

Bush would like to get our minds off Iraq by attacking Iran. That way, he could get one more war under his belt. Go get him, Joe Biden!

Meanwhile, we wander around aimlessly, homeless in paradise, waiting for the other shoe to drop.

Whatever Happened to the "Class Struggle"?

Class Struggle. Now, there's an expression with clout. You don't hear it much, anymore. Don't fool yourself. It's there. It's like an underground stream. It surfaces now and then.

You can call it the war between the haves and the have-nots. It's been going on since the beginning of human endeavor. But it was Karl Marx and Friedrich Engels who pinned it down. "The history of all hitherto existing society is the history of class struggle," they said.

There are nodal points in history, called revolutions. The industrial revolution, the French Revolution, the Russian Revolution, were nodal points, where quantitative change turned to qualitative change, where political and economic systems that no longer met the needs of people changed to fit the new conditions. The slave system to feudalism. Feudalism to Capitalism. Capitalism to --?

Marx defined an economic class by its relationship to the means of production—its position in the social structure that characterizes capitalism—two classes, the *proletariat* and the *bourgeoisie*, otherwise known as the working class and the capitalist class.

In a free labor system, under capitalism, you pay your worker a wage (that represents only a part payment for the value he produces). You have only to extract the surplus value that the worker contributes to the making of the product. You call it profit and say it is derived from entrepreneurial skill, reward for taking risks, from the machinery, the land, or other such gibberish. Once you extract the surplus value the worker creates, let him be free to go his own way and the devil take the hindmost. There is always a plentiful supply of labor to be had.

That's not the end of the story. What happens is that eventually, the worker wises up and starts to demand the full value of his work, or maybe settle for a larger slice of the pie. That's when the fur begins to fly. That's called the class struggle.

Throughout economic history that struggle has gone on. It's an old, old fight between the haves and the have-nots. It pushes capital on to heights of glory, monopoly and war. We're in such a period right now.

We need to keep production high and labor costs low to keep the system afloat, they tell us. The EPA notwithstanding, production and profits trump the environment. Take a look at us now. Shop until you drop, the propaganda organs shout. "But with what?" asks the underpaid and the unemployed. The productivity of labor is at its height. The purchasing power of the working class is low.

Under capitalism, the assault on labor has been overwhelming, continuous, inhuman and destructive from the beginning of the industrial revolution to this very day. No wonder unions are dysfunctional and chaotic. So are most of their leaders. If they're not coerced, co-opted or corrupted, they're framed, jailed or neutralized in some way. Only when capitalism is in the throes of crisis, deep depression and near collapse can labor leaders like Eugene V. Debs or John L. Lewis emerge.

Debs organized the American Railway Union, an industrial union for all railroad workers in 1893, became a confirmed Socialist while serving time in prison for refusing to comply with a federal court injunction, ran for President of the United States four times on the Socialist Party ticket, the last time from prison in 1920 and received nearly 1 million votes.

John L. Lewis led the United Mine Workers in organizing most of the coal industry, was one of the organizers of the Congress of Industrial Organizations (CIO) in 1936 and joined the Reuther brothers, Walter and Victor, in organizing the United Auto Workers' sit-down strikes against General Motors at their Flint, Michigan plants.

For 44 bitterly cold winter days the auto workers in Flint held out, eventually inspiring more than two-thirds of General Motors 145 thousand other production workers to strike as well, at dozens of other plants. The strikers in Flint seized, shut down and occupied one, then two, and then three of the key GM plants. Suddenly, workers everywhere were sitting-down. There were 477 sitdown strikes by the end of 1937, involving more than half a million workers.

Mighty GM had vowed publicly that it would never allow the UAW to represent its employees. But the General Motors Corporation ended up granting that crucial right—and more—to the union. It was a stunning victory for the United Auto Workers. It led the way—and swiftly—to the unionization of workers throughout heavy industry and, ultimately, to unionization in all fields. It certainly was the high water mark of labor power in America.

The class struggle goes on. One day, it will reach a turning point, again. With computers and digital technology, a planned economy is not only more feasible but inevitable in a future socialist society.

It took capitalism four hundred years to hone its skills. It's a trial and error process. The system served its purpose and is now ready to leave the stage of history, or "dig its own grave" if you prefer Marx's expression. There's a new one waiting in the wings. Socialism. Only been around about a century. Made a couple of mistakes but learning.

The Greening of the Oligarchy

America's Byzantine campaign financing system is like the slave auction block in days of yore.

As a corporate finagler, you buy and pay for your politician and put him to work for your corporation or in your industry's behalf. A good day's pay for a good day's work. The American way.

Everybody knows that most politicians are in some corporate pocket or beholden to some special interest, a mélange of corruption and cronyism. When Ike Eisenhower, our hero of World War II and two-term President left office in 1961, he warned the citizens of this nation, "Beware the Military-Industrial Complex". Obviously, we didn't heed the warning.

For the last, long, four years, our Military-Industrial-Privatized Mercenary Security Corporations have been sopping up billions of our taxpayer dollars. Our criminally inclined President Bush and the oligarchy he represents, has kept a meaningless war going in Iraq. Our former head of the Federal Reserve, Alan Greenspan, a long-time tool of the oligarchy, now tells us it does have a meaning. He says this war is about oil. An interesting admission on his part, but not the whole story.

He knows, as well as everybody else, that this war is also about corporate profits, the destruction of democracy in America – and death.

No one seems to know how to save themselves and the nation. The laxity is especially pernicious in the Congress of the United States. They talk about "exit strategy" but everybody has a different time-line for when to get out. Except for Dennis Kucinich who says, "Get out now".

The representatives of the people are supposed to serve the people of this nation—not Norman Hsu, an alleged Hong-Kong apparel mogul, about whom presidential candidate, Senator Hillary Clinton, was embarrassed enough to refund a total of $850,000 in bundled contributions she received from this benefactor… and his bundling associate, Winkle Paw.

Or was it Senator Joe Lieberman of Connecticut who collected $197,000 in campaign contributions from the insurance industry? His wife, Hadassah, works as a lobbyist for the pharmaceutical industry so he gets it both ways.

It's not just Democrats or former Democrats. Republicans are equal opportunity scroungers.

Rudy Giuliani, former Mayor of New York City, and presently presumed front runner for the Republican primary in the 2008 presidential race, has tapped into the Bush family's Texas connections and Big Oil billionaires, as Ari Berman reveals in the current issue of *The Nation Magazine* (10/29/07)

Rudy is now a partner in the Houston law firm of Bracewell & Giuliani LLP. The firm has more than 400 lawyers in offices in a half dozen cities in the US as well as overseas in Dubai, London and Kazakhstan. The firm's area of specialization includes energy, banking, environmental strategies and especially noteworthy, white-collar criminal defense.

Ari Berman rounds out the picture. Bracewell's clients have included massive coal-burning power plants like the Atlanta-based Southern

Company; more than 450 oil companies represented by the National Petrochemical and Refiners Association and Texas heavy hitters like Enron, ChevronTexaco and Valero Energy. All these interests had a major stake in persuading George W. Bush to abandon his campaign pledge to regulate carbon dioxide, the leading source of green-house gas emissions... Partner Giuliani now wants to become President Giuliani.

And so it goes...with our elected representatives. What can we do about it? Senators McCain and Feingold made a stab at it in 2002 with their Bipartisan Campaign Reform Act (BCRA).

The Act became the law of the land. But it was a paper tiger. One of its goals was to control *soft money* in campaign financing. Soft money are funds spent by organizations that are not contributed directly to candidate campaigns and which do not "expressly advocate" the election or defeat of a candidate.

Candidates get around this by "bundling", the practice of one donor gathering donations from many different individuals and presenting the sum to a campaign.

Public funding is available but those who do accept it are subject to spending limits. The amounts are puny compared to the filthy lucre needed in today's highly charged campaigns. It's rumored that Hillary has already corralled about $35 million and that's only for the Democratic primary campaign. So the bidding is still open. Hillary and the other candidates are still on the block. Elections can no longer be called "democracy's feast".

But where's the fix?

The subject is debated endlessly, on the left and on the right and in the center. The spin goes on, twirling the same, safe issues—the war, health insurance, immigration, abortion, gay marriage, prayer in schools...

even the economy. In the earlier Bill Clinton campaigns, James Carville, the "Ragin' Cajun", one of Clinton's flacks, came up with a neat slogan— "It's the economy, Stupid!" It may have won Bill the election.

In the present campaign, I haven't heard any candidate say, "It's the system, Stupid!" However, you do hear a mention, now and then, about the depredations of capitalism in the mass media. Is there a shift in the tectonic plates? Not much of one. One swallow doesn't a summer make. Capitalism, like Israeli policy, is a taboo subject in the fearful lexicon of most newspaper editors, radio and TV program managers.

In our national security interest, a little debate about our moribund system might be helpful. Speak truth to power. What power? Corporate power.

Go back in history and get it from the horse's mouth. What horse? Benito Mussolini, the pre-World War II dictator of fascist Italy. He coined the word Fascism and he defined it as Corporatism. When corporations take over the government, by whatever means, that's Fascism, said Benito. Wealth flows up to the few. Misery flows down to the many.

Tax cuts for the rich. Welfare for the corporations. George Bush and Dick Cheney are very good at providing that. Through them and their cronies, the corporadoes are running the government and its foreign policy.

If a Democratic regime makes it to power in 2008, will it change much?

Aren't you sick and tired, yet, of voting for the evil of two lessers? No, there's not a dime's worth of difference between the two parties—maybe a cent's worth. Either way, the capitalist system leads to oligarchy. And oligarchy trumps democracy.

So, let's talk about the stupid system, shall we?

The Rain of Riches

In December, 2006, Goldman Sachs, a Wall Street financial services company, announced a sixteen and a half billion dollar bonus for its 26,500 employees, an average of $623,418 per employee. Their newly appointed CEO received a bonus of $52,000,000.

With the rain of riches falling upon Wall Street these days, the practice of distributing rewards at the top is picking up steam. CEOs and executives at Lehman Brothers and Morgan Stanley are receiving bonuses as high as $60 million. The manna from heaven continues to fall, and the optimists just want to let the good times roll. They see the benefits of Capitalism unending. Halleluiah! We're on a bonus march!

The very thought of it takes your breath away and also takes you back to the days of the original bonus marchers.

In May of 1924, the US Congress voted a cash bonus to the veterans of World War I. Because the money wasn't readily at hand, they devised a delayed bonus structure, the money to be paid out in twenty years, around 1944 and 1945.

But in the spring and summer of 1932, in the depth of the "unexpected" Great Depression, the veterans petitioned the government for part payment of their bonuses to provide some relief for those whose jobs and income took a dive as a result of the collapsed economy.

Although the Congress went along with the idea and passed a bill that would allow veterans to borrow up to 50% of the certificate value of their bonuses, then Republican President Herbert Hoover, not being a big "tax and spend" man, vetoed the bill.

This raised hell with the veterans. Led by Walter W. Waters, a former Army petty officer, 60,000 World War I vets, many with their families, descended on Washington from across the country. They massed at the Capitol building and threw together improvised camps around the city that came to be known as *Hoovervilles*, the largest of which was in Anacostia Flats, a swampy area not far from downtown Washington. >From these encampments they harassed the government relentlessly for payment of their bonuses.

The harassment did not last long. The Hoover Administration panicked. This was Bolshevik time and they saw the hairy hand of communism in a raised fist.

The Washington police attempted to remove some Bonus Army protesters from a federal construction site. The police fatally shot two veterans in the process and the protesters retaliated with blunt weapons, wounding several police and a riot ensued.

This made the District of Columbia commissioners very antsy. They notified Hoover that they could no longer maintain the peace, whereupon Hoover ordered federal troops in to remove the marchers from the general area.

And who were the officers to whom Hoover entrusted this job? No less than the future heroes of World War II. Under the overall command of General Douglas MacArthur, the marchers were cleared and their camps destroyed by George S. Patton, then a Major from

Fort Myer, and Dwight D. Eisenhower, a member of MacArthur's staff.

They sent in troops with tear gas and bayonets drawn. They marched their troops across the Anacostia River, into the largest of the veteran protesters' encampments. The protesters were given the moniker of "Bonus Expeditionary Force" to lay on them some kind of pejorative image of an imperial army come to do battle. The government troops burned down the veterans' tents and shacks; cleared and destroyed their camps. Thousands of veterans were driven out of town, many were injured, and two were killed. Two infants died from gas asphyxiation, an eleven year old boy was partially blinded by tear gas, one bystander was shot in the shoulder and one veteran's ear was severed by a Cavalry saber. Twelve police were injured. More than 1000 men, women and children were exposed to the tear gas. This might not sound too bad for the amount of havoc that was wrought, but as much as anything else, it landed Herbert Hoover's image in the gutter.

Hoover's side of the story turned up, years later, in his memoir published by The Macmillan Company in 1952. Hoover says:

"…many Democratic speakers in the (Presidential) campaign of 1932 implied that I had murdered veterans on the streets of Washington. As abundantly proved later on, the march was, in considerable part, organized and promoted by the Communists and included a large number of hoodlums and ex-convicts determined to raise a public disturbance it was of interest to learn in after years from the Communist confessions that they also had put on a special battery of speakers to help Roosevelt in his campaign by use of this incident."

Sound familiar? Where have we heard that kind of rationale before? Could it have been from the Bush Administration—if you substitute the word "terrorist" for "Communist"?

The operative word here may be "Capitalism". Its nature is to boom and bust.

The system allows for the kind of conditions that produced both the bonuses distributed by Goldman Sachs in December of 2006 and the fight for theirs by the veteran protesters in the bonus marches of 1932. There have been many changes in the nature of capitalism in those intervening years. If Karl Marx were alive and well today, and living in America, he might not even recognize the economic system that he critiqued and analyzed in *Das Kapital,* when he wrote it in 1867. It wasn't a bad call. Starting with primitive capital accumulation to feed the Industrial Revolution, small commodity production developed. It was a snowball rolling down hill. Mergers and acquisitions were the inevitable result. Monopoly, imperialism and war followed, stimulated by the grab for raw materials from less developed areas around the world. The creation of surplus value and profit, of course, was the key to it all. Marx might not have believed the working class would have allowed it to have gotten this bad. The amount of profit being raked in by the corporate class is obscene. It certainly would have boggled his mind.

The coming world economic crisis is long past due. It wouldn't be just a stock market crash. It would be the total collapse of the house-of-cards still called "capitalism" today. All that is needed is a single spark-like China calling in its paper-the debt that the US has accumulated to finance the Iraq war and other catastrophes.

When the collapse comes, the question is, will there be enough time and enough of the natural world left to start rebuilding a new kind of society that has been demonized for generations called "socialism".

Afterword

Who I Am

Stephen Fleischman's career as a documentary writer-director-producer spans more than three decades -- 10 years with CBS NEWS, 20 years with ABC NEWS -- independent documentary production and writing for television.

His final program for ABC NEWS was THE COCAINE CARTEL, a one-hour investigative report for the CLOSEUP series. He took a film crew to Medellin, Colombia, the cocaine capitol of the world. The program named and reported on the five largest and most dangerous drug traffickers. When THE COCAINE CARTEL aired on the ABC Network it sent shock waves through the drug world from Miami to Bogotá.

Fleischman began his television career at CBS NEWS as writer and story editor in 1953. He worked with Irving Gitlin's Public Affairs unit on the award-winning series, THE SEARCH, an examination of research projects at America's leading universities. He was then named producer of the children's program, LET'S TAKE A TRIP, hosted by Sonny Fox, which gained wide acclaim. He went on to produce THE AMERICAN CHALLENGE with Eric Severeid as host -- and in 1957-

58 was producer of hour-long special programs in Walter Cronkite's THE TWENTIETH CENTURY series that captured a number of EMMY AWARDS.

In 1959, Fleischman participated in the formation of the renowned Murrow-Friendly CBS REPORTS series. Fleischman's first assignment as Producer-Director was NIGERIA - THE FREEDOM EXPLOSION, a program that chronicled the birth of that nation in 1960. It won an OVERSEAS PRESS CLUB AWARD for Fleischman and Eric Severeid, the correspondent on the program.

Fleischman continued to write, produce and direct CBS REPORTS programs for the next five years. They included THE BUSINESS OF HEALTH: MONEY, MEDICINE AND POLITICS with Correspondent Howard K. Smith, a scrutiny of the controversies that raged around the health care issues of the time. Fleischman's BIRTH CONTROL AND THE LAW won the coveted ALBERT AND MARY LASKER MEDICAL JOURNALISM AWARD for 1962. It was the first program of its kind to deal candidly, and in depth, with the social, moral and legal controversies over birth control and the new FDA-approved birth control pill. CBS REPORTS: THE HARLEM TEMPER, in 1963, was the first treatment of the rising Black Nationalist movement with extensive coverage of the role of Malcolm X.

In 1964, ABC NEWS President, Elmer Lower, brought Fleischman to the burgeoning News Division of the American Broadcasting Companies where Fleischman established his own Documentary Unit.

For the next ten years, as Producer and Executive Producer, he turned out three to four one-hour and two-hour specials a year that won a number of awards. In 1964, THE GREAT DIVIDE: CIVIL RIGHTS AND THE BILL caught the turmoil of the Civil Rights struggle of the time. That year, he also produced MAN INVADES THE SEA, with the participation of Astronaut Scott Carpenter and WE ARE NOT ALONE with New York Times Science Reporter, Walter Sullivan.

With the escalation of the Vietnam War in1965, Fleischman went to Vietnam with Correspondent Edward P. Morgan to produce a documentary on our role there. The result was a one hour program entitled THE AGONY OF VIETNAM. When telecast in August of 1965 it raised a storm of controversy -- hailed by anti-war forces for its objectivity, criticized in government circles because it did support US policy on the war.

Fleischman continued to produce documentaries dealing with science and medicine, cultural and social themes. The year 1966 saw the beginning of a series of four hour-long documentaries on American music, the first of which was THE ANATOMY OF POP: THE MUSIC EXPLOSION. It has had repeated telecasts on the ABC Network and in syndication. In that year, as a special request of ABC Board Chairman, Leonard Goldenson, Fleischman was asked to produce a Public Service program on the subject of retardation in children. THE LONG CHILDHOOD OF TIMMY was the result. The program focused on the personal story of a Downs Syndrome child and his loving family. It won Fleischman a second LASKER MEDICAL JOURNALISM AWARD.

The years 1969 and 1970 saw the dawning, in the American consciousness, of pollution problems threatening this country. In those years, Fleischman produced a three-part series called MISSION POSSIBLE and a two-hour special, THREE YOUNG AMERICANS IN SEARCH OF SURVIVAL, narrated by Paul Newman, on the subject of ecological and environmental problems. They were the first in-depth studies of this subject on network television. In 1970, another corporate request, an ABC NEWS gift to UNICEF, was assigned to Fleischman. The documentary special TO ALL THE WORLD'S CHILDREN, took him to three continents, to Paraguay, to Kenya and to Sri Lanka (Ceylon) to show UNICEF's work in the context of national and cultural influences on children. The program is narrated by film actor Rod Steiger and is still in exhibition at the UN.

By 1973, the ABC NEWS commitment to the television documentary took another leap.

The individual production units were merged into ABC NEWS CLOSEUP, a regularly scheduled monthly documentary series under the aegis of Av Westin. Fleischman continued to function as writer-director-producer on the series for the next ten years.

Some of his notable contributions -- WEST VIRGINIA: LIFE, LIBERTY AND THE PURSUIT OF COAL, the premiere program, broke new ground in setting the form and style for the series. It garnered an EMMY AWARD for CLOSEUP. The following year OIL: THE POLICY CRISIS with Correspondent Brit Hume brought a different viewpoint to the so-called "energy crisis" of 1974. In that year, too, CLOSEUP ON HOFFA, an investigative biography with unusual access to the man, sharpened the focus on Jimmy Hoffa, Frank Fitzsimmons, the Teamsters' Union and its connections to government and organized crime. It was cited for excellence in investigative reporting.

In 1975, Fleischman's investigative report, THE CIA, anticipated the conclusions of the highly critical Rockefeller Commission findings that were released later that year. Other investigative reports on consumerism and fraud followed.

The 1979 NEW YORK STATE BROADCASTERS AWARD went to Fleischman's NOBODY'S CHILDREN, a penetrating revelation of foster care and adoption scandals in New York, Chicago and New Orleans.

In the 1980's, Fleischman produced documentaries on penology, science and politics, and another program on the United Nations, its peacekeeping and refugee relief missions. This took him to the refugee camps in Honduras and to the firing line with UNIFIL troops in Lebanon in 1982, on the eve of the Israeli invasion of that country.

Fleischman's career at ABC NEWS was capped in 1983 with the prestigious COLUMBIA UNIVERSITY-DUPONT TELEVISION JOURNALISM AWARD for his CLOSEUP: THE GENE MERCHANTS. This was the first television exploration of DNA and the new science of gene splicing and its ethical and economic ramifications for society.

In the later part of the 80's, Fleischman worked with Yue-Sai Kan, Executive Producer and Host of the cable television series LOOKING EAST. The programs, aired on the SPN cable network, were designed to convey a better understanding of the Far East to American audiences. Miss Kan was also awarded a contract by CCTV, the television network of the People's Republic of China, to produce 52 15-minute programs to explain the rest of the world to Chinese audiences. Fleischman, who traveled with Miss Kan and a videotape crew to South America and Europe, wrote and directed a number of these programs. The series, entitled ONE WORLD, was dubbed in Mandarin and English and both versions were telecast twice throughout the People's Republic before the Tiananmen Square events of 1989.

In recent years, Fleischman has devoted himself to writing fiction and non-fiction, much of it based on his experiences in network news. Forty of Mr. Fleischman's documentaries are in the collection and archives of THE MUSEUM OF TELEVISION AND RADIO in New York and Los Angeles.

Stephen Fleischman is a member of the Directors Guild of America, Inc. and a *Lifetime Current Member* of the Writers Guild of America, East, Inc. He is a graduate of *Haverford College*, Class of 1940, with a Bachelor of Arts degree and is presently living in Los Angeles with his wife, Dede Allen, a life-long feature film editor.

Documentography

The documentaries of Stephen Fleischman in the collection and archives of The Paley Center for Media (formerly the Museum of Television and Radio) available for screening in New York and Beverly Hills.

1. **CORNELL: AUTO SAFETY RESEARCH** 1953 (black and white) one half hour with Walter Cronkite THE SEARCH series
CBS NEWS Public Affairs

2. **ARKANSAS: FOLKLORE RESEARCH** 1954 (black and white) one half hour with Charles Romaine THE SEARCH series
CBS NEWS Public Affairs

3. **THE FACE OF CRIME** 1958 (black and white) one hour with Walter Cronkite THE TWENTIETH CENTURY series
CBS NEWS Public Affairs

4. **GENERATION WITHOUT A CAUSE** 1959
Part 1 **Self Portrait** (black and white) one half hour
Part 2 **The Searchers** (black and white) one half hour
THE TWENTIETH CENTURY series with Walter Cronkite
CBS NEWS Public Affairs

5. **NIGERIA: THE FREEDOM EXPLOSION** 1960 (black and white) one hour with Eric Sevareid
CBS Reports, CBS NEWS

6. **THE GREAT FARM VOTE OF '63** 1963 (black and white one hour with Harry Reasoner
CBS Reports, CBS NEWS

7. **THE GREAT DIVIDE: CIVIL RIGHTS AND THE BILL** 1964 (black and white) onehour with Bob Young
ABC NEWS DOCUMENTARY UNIT

8. **JFK: HIS TWO WORLDS** 1964 (black & white) one hour with Bill Downs, Bill Lawrence and Edward P. Morgan
ABC NEWS DOCUMENTARY UNIT

9. THE AGONY OF VIETNAM 1965 (black & white) one hour with Edward P. Morgan
ABC NEWS DOCUMENTARY UNIT

10. MAN INVADES THE SEA 1965 (black and white) one hour with Robert Montgomery
ABC NEWS DOCUMENTARY UNIT

11. EVERYBODY'S GOT A SYSTEM 1965 (black and white) one hour with Terry Thomas.
ABC NEWS DOCUMENTARY UNIT

12. ANATOMY OF POP: The Music Explosion 1966 (black and white) one-hour with Bob Young
ABC NEWS DOCUMENTARY UNIT

13. THE BAFFLING WORLD OF ESP 1966 (black and white) one hour with Basil Rathbone
ABC NEWS DOCUMENTARY UNIT

14. WE ARE NOT ALONE 1966 (black and white) one hour with **NEW YORK TIMES** Science Editor, Walter Sullivan
ABC NEWS DOCUMENTARY UNIT

15. THE LONG CHILDHOOD OF TIMMY 1966 (black and white) one hour with E.G. Marshall
ABC NEWS DOCUMENTARY UNIT

16. RIDDLE OF THE MAYAN CAVE 1967 (black and white) one hour with the EXPLORERS CLUB
ABC NEWS DOCUMENTARY UNIT

17. ONE NIGHT STANDS 1967 (color) (Woody Herman's Herd, Johnny Rivers, the Bartok Circus) one hour with Bing Crosby
ABC NEWS DOCUMENTARY UNIT

18. THE SONG MAKERS 1968 (color) one hour with Narrator Joel Crager
ABC NEWS DOCUMENTARY UNIT

19. THE SINGERS 1969 (color) one hour with Gloria Loring and Aretha Franklin
ABC NEWS DOCUMENTARY UNIT

20. ATLANTA: It Can Be Done 1969 (color) one hour
ABC NEWS DOCUMENTARY UNIT

21. BLACK FIDDLER: Prejudice and the Negro 1969 (color) one hour
ABC NEWS DOCUMENTARY UNIT

22. THREE YOUNG AMERICANS IN SEARCH OF SURVIVAL 1969 (color)
two hours with Paul Newman
ABC NEWS DOCUMENTARY UNIT

23. TO ALL THE WORLD'S CHILDREN 1970 (color) one hour for UNICEF
with Rod Steiger
ABC NEWS DOCUMENTARY UNIT

24. MISSION POSSIBLE: Part One They Care For A City 1970 (San
Francisco) (color) one hour with Colonel Frank Borman
ABC NEWS DOCUMENTARY UNIT

25. MISSION POSSIBLE: Part Two They Care for the Land 1969 (color) one
hour with Colonel Frank Borman
ABC NEWS DOCUMENTART UNIT

26. MISSION POSSIBLE: Part Three They Care For A Nation 1970 (color)
one hour with Colonel Frank Borman
ABC NEWS DOCUMENTARY UNIT

27. THE CHEROKEE SHAFT: The Story of Mines and Men 1971 (color) one
hour with Frank Reynolds
ABC NEWS DOCUMENTARY UNIT

28. ASSAULT ON PRIVACY 1972 (color) one hour with Frank Reynolds
ABC NEWS DOCUMENTARY UNIT

29. OCEANS: The Silent Crisis 1972 (color) one hour
ABC NEWS DOCUMENTARY UNIT

30. THE YOUNG CONVICTS: Prison in the Streets 1972 (color) one hour
with Frank Reynolds
ABC NEWS DOCUMENTARY UNIT

31. THE BUILDING INNOVATORS 1973 (color) one hour with Frank Reynolds
ABC NEWS DOCUMENTARY UNIT

32. WEST VIRGINIA: LIFE, LIBERTY AND THE PURSUIT OF COAL 1973
(color) one hour with Jim Kincaid and Brit Hume
ABC NEWS CLOSEUP

33. HOFFA 1974 (color) one hour An investigative biography of former
Teamster President James R. Hoffa with Jim Kincaid, Bill Gill and Brit Hume
ABC NEWS CLOSEUP

34. MEDICINE AND MONEY 1976 (color) one hour with Frank Reynolds
ABC NEWS CLOSEUP

35. ERA: The War Between the Women 1977 (color) one hour with Howard
K. Smith
ABC NEWS CLOSEUP

36. NOBODY'S CHILDREN 1979 (color) one hour with Brit Hume
ABC NEWS CLOSEUP

37. DEATH IN A SOUTHWEST PRISON 1980 (color) one hour with Tom Jarrell
ABC NEWS CLOSEUP

38. THE GENE MERCHANTS 1981 (color) one hour with Marshall Frady
ABC NEWS CLOSEUP

39. THE COCAINE CARTEL 1983 (color) one hour with Bill Redeker
ABC NEWS CLOSEUP

40. PRISON GROUP THERAPY (Bordentown Reformatory, New Jersey)
Supplement to THE TWENTIETH CENTURY series special **The Face of Crime**
1958 (black and white) two hours
CBS NEWS